AMERICAN BICYCLE RACING

AMERICAN BICYCLE RACING

Edited By
JAMES C. MCCULLAGH

With Contributions From
DICK SWANN
DAVE CHAUNER
ALICE KOVLER, Velo-News
OWEN MULHOLLAND

RODALE PRESS, INC.
EMMAUS, PENNA.

Printed in the United States of America on recycled paper

Library of Congress Cataloging in Publication Data
Main entry under title:

American bicycle racing.

   Bibliography: p.
   Includes index.
   1. Bicycle racing—United States—History.
I. Swann, Dick. II. McCullagh, James C.
GV1049.A48   796.6   76-26088

                ISBN 0-87857-144-2

        2   4   6   8   10   9   7   5   3   1

Contents

Acknowledgments

I would like to thank Alf Goullet, Jimmy Walthour, Victor Linart, and Torchy Pedem, great racers from the past, who provided fresh and valuable information about their many seasons of racing. My thanks to Jack Simes for his discussions of the contemporary racing scene, especially the Six-Day.

I would like to thank *American Motorcyclist and Bicyclist* for making their valuable collections available to me; Stephen Greene Press, Inc., for permission to publish excerpts from *The Fastest Bicycle Rider in the World;* Mrs. Sydney Taylor Brown, for permission to publish one of her father's letters; the "Pop" Brennan bike shop of Irvington, New Jersey, who provided me with priceless scrapbooks and photo albums; *Velo-News* for permission to publish an excerpt from *Bicycle Racing;* and Alice Bahr for her tireless research.

My thanks also to the individual contributors for their great cooperation.

James C. McCullagh

Introduction

Seventy years ago the most popular spectator sport in America was bicycle racing. Crowds of up to 30,000 attended professional and amateur races in Worchester, Massachusetts; Ottumwa, Iowa; and Peoria, Illinois. In fact, there were more than a hundred bicycle tracks or velodromes scattered across the country. Few communities did not have a track of gravel, cinders, cement, dirt, or wood. Road and track racing permeated every aspect of life. Highly paid professional riders caught the fancy of the public and were idolized in America, Europe, and Australia. Arthur Zimmerman, Major Taylor, and Frank Kramer were international heroes.

At the other end of the spectrum were amateur and club riders who guaranteed that racing was a grass-roots sport. Rare was the county fair or bazaar without a bike race as a part of the program. Rare was the school which did not give over some time to racing.

The refinement of the bicycle late in the nineteenth century was a major factor in the bike racing boom. Racing represented a daring and spectacular application of a new machine at the bitter edge of man's ability. Society, thrilled by the bicycle, was eager to participate in stunning and often reckless races against time and distance. The bicycle allowed for astonishing human performances.

Once considered the mecca of track sports, America lost interest in racing in the 1930s. But in recent years the bicycle has made a remarkable recovery, promising to outnumber the car by 1980. Concurrently, Americans are witnessing a renewed interest in bicycle racing, particularly on the track. Velodromes are being constructed in many parts of the country. Colleges and high schools are establishing racing programs as part of the sports curriculum.

Spearheading this recovery are the accomplishments of men and women racers in international competition. At the 1975 Pan-American Games in Mexico City, the American track team won four of the 12 medals awarded. According to Jack Simes, Pan-American and Olympic track coach, "We did it for the sport. We wanted to show Americans that track racing is worth watching and supporting." This feat, coupled with the medals won in Worlds competition by Sue Novara, Sheila Young, and Mary Jane Reoch, suggests that America has some of the most promising track riders in the world.

The proposition that bicycle racing is an ideal sport for spectators and participants alike is the central idea of this book. There is a place for everyone along the exciting continuum of racing and leisure riding. The primary emphasis of the book is to demonstrate that bicycle racing in America has an illustrious past, an exciting present, and a promising future. Our focus is on the human side of the sport, on the heroes and heroines whose magnificent achievements represent one of the finest chapters in American sports history. We have examined bicycle racing, particularly the Six-Day and Motor Pacing, through interviews with Jimmy Walthour, Alf Goullet, and Victor Linart. We discuss road and track events, techniques of racing, and the psychologies of the racers. We explore the European racing scene in detail and its relationship to American racing. Through photographs, interviews, letters, magazine and newspaper accounts, and personal observations, we hope we have captured the essence of bicycle racing in America.

CHAPTER ONE

Bicycle Racing: The Early Years

DICK SWANN and JAMES C. MC CULLAGH

LATE in the nineteenth century Americans rediscovered the wheel, mainly in the form of bicycles and tricycles. Considering that the wheel was "discovered" some 5,000 years ago, it is all the more remarkable that it took so long for many to give it serious attention. And, as is often the case, few realized the potential of the invention until years later.

In 1818, many a Londoner was startled by a middle-aged gentleman who balanced himself uneasily on a wooden frame fitted with two heavy wheels. The gentleman was riding a pedestrian hobby horse which he propelled by pushing his feet. If he was lucky, he could travel up to 10 miles an hour and 50 miles in a day. Although the cartoonists ridiculed the hobby horse, it represented a real breakthrough.

Approximately 50 years later the hobby horse gave way to the vélocipède, or "bone-shaker," made of heavy iron and wood. It was driven by pedals on the front wheel and had a brake on the back wheel operated by a twist-grip on the handlebars. Even though the "bone-shaker" was cumbersome and difficult to ride, it was used in many bicycle races in England and France.

The high-wheeler (also called the penny farthing or ordinary), with its direct-drive front wheel, tubular steel frames, and spoked wheels, was a great improvement over previous bicycles. Nonetheless, mounting and riding an ordinary was no easy matter as you would have to put your left foot on the back rest and hop along until you got up enough speed. Only then could you jump in the saddle, six feet high. Not surprisingly, ordinaries contributed to many a broken leg and neck. Surprisingly, speeds of up to 20 miles an hour were reached.

With the invention of the safety bicycle in 1884, the cycle begins its modern history. In fact the safety bicycle, noted for its chain-driven rear wheel, pneumatic tire, and relatively light weight, is very close in design to the present-day bicycle.

The introduction of the bicycle to Americans of all classes represented nothing less than a social revolution. Bicycle instruction schools were common in cities and towns. Bicycle manufacturing became big business. In 1896 there were 1,200 bicycle makers in New York and 83 bicycle shops within a radius of a mile.

The newspapers were filled with accounts of the strange activities of cyclists. Bicycles were used by highway robbers, by policemen in Philadelphia, and by post office workers in many cities. Before long, the army became interested in the machine. Accordingly, a folding bike was invented, as well as one which could accommodate a machine gun. Army generals sent relays of riders across country to test their speed and endurance.

Bicycles touched every corner of American life. Rarely a day went by without an account of a new technological application of the bicycle. Bikes were adapted for use on rails, on fences, even on the ice. One man invented a wind-driven bicycle.

Naturally, with so much social, technological, and human interest in the machine, attention was soon turned to the racing potential of the bicycle. Organized and spontaneous races were held at fairgrounds, on trotting and dirt tracks, and occasionally indoors where bicycle riders would race on the outside of a roller skating rink.

America went mad with the bicycle. As early as 1881, cyclists could be seen riding ordinaries on the Schuylkill River, near Philadelphia in the wintertime. Trips were made from Philadelphia to Trenton on the frozen Delaware. In 1897 a cyclist and an ice skater held a race in Reading, Pennsylvania, which the cyclist won.

U. S. Bureau of Public Roads
Photo No. 30-N-40-3431

A celebrated description of a bone-shaker riding school in New York in 1869.

U. S. Bureau of Public Roads
Photo No. 34-N-2366

The safety bicycle was adapted to railroad tracks and special steel-track bicycle paths.

Thousands of Americans belonged to touring clubs which strenuously pushed for better roads. In 1896 three members of a New York touring club each rode over 10,000 miles, which is a very good figure even today.

Although the first riders tended to be gentlemen amateurs, mass production rapidly brought the bicycle within the means of all those who desired one. For the first time people had a mobility limited only by their muscles and the state of the roads. Then as now, the bicycle was also part of the fresh air movement, especially for women. Importantly, it was used to introduce women to outdoor sport.

American Firsts

The first true bicycle racer in America was the gentleman amateur who worked all week and donned his racing jersey on a Saturday afternoon and competed at the county fair. Because the horse was still supreme, the cyclist took his place behind the trotters. These racers rode for pleasure. At that time professionalism in sport was frowned upon.

On May 24, 1878, the first bicycle race in America was held at Beacon Park in Boston. It was won by C. A. Parker of Harvard University. He won the three-mile race in 12 minutes 27 seconds. Boston can justly claim to be the cradle of American cycling. The first bicycle dealers in the United States were Cunningham Heath & Co. of Boston, founded in 1877. The first all-cycling newspaper, *Bicycling World*, was born in Boston in the same year. The first cycling club in the country was the Boston Bicycling Club, formed in 1878 and still active.

The early bicycle races were memorable, and sometimes dangerous affairs, usually held wherever the particular club could find room. It was natural that for the first few years racing men competed largely on trotting tracks which were not prepared in advance. But in 1882 a special board track was constructed in the New England Industrial Fair Building in Boston. Ralph P. Ahl, a strong Boston rider, was the first American to ride a mile in under three minutes. The race against the clock had begun.

Two years later, H. E. Ducker, the P. T. Barnum of cycle racing, sought to put America on the racing map. He conceived the

Participants in one of America's first bicycle tours line up with their ordinaries outside of Readville, Massachusetts, September 11, 1879.

The ordinary and the safety. By 1893 the ordinary was on the way out, to be followed by the solid tire safety or low front wheel model.

A touring club from Hagerstown, Maryland getting ready for a ride in the early 1890s. The flags indicate the riders were probably participating in a local holiday celebration.

idea of building a special bicycle track inside the Hampden Park trotting track in Springfield, Massachusetts. With the help of the best civil engineers in America and Europe, he helped make track building a science and helped make track racing an exciting spectator sport. During a three-day meet at Springfield, all American and European records were wiped out. The cycling world was astonished.

The record for the mile was reduced from three minutes twenty seconds to less than two-and-a-half minutes. The times were so remarkable that the English press refused to print them. Equally important, track racing had seized the imagination of America. On the first day 9,000 people attended. When the word got out about the record-shattering performances, 18,000 attended the next day. It was not uncommon for towns such as Hartford and Springfield to close down entirely from noon until sunset on a racing day.

In these days of the supersonic transport, it is sometimes difficult to understand that man can be tied so closely to the conquest of time as he was in the 1890s. Perhaps the last time the breaking of the time barrier attracted such attention was in 1954, when the Englishman Roger Bannister broke the four-minute mile. As early as 1892 the mile had been run in about four minutes and twelve seconds. Surprisingly, it took close to 60 years to reduce the time to below the four-minute barrier.

But in the last decade of the nineteenth century, bicycle speed records seemed to tumble by the day. Man felt he could perform any feat with the machine. The bicycle liberated him to try the impossible.

On the other hand, many saw the bicycle as a symbol of the mechanization of life. Some feared that the rider and the racer would put an end to the glorious history of the horse. America was alive with talk of the bicycle and the trotter. The horsemen in particular were concerned over the possibility of the steed of blood and bone being outdistanced by the "steed of steel."

Newspaper writers were astonished by the record-breaking feats of the riders. When John S. Johnson rode a mile on a safety bike, paced part of the way by a running horse, in under two minutes, writers proclaimed that America was entering a new age.

Smithsonian Institution

Professional riders preparing for a race in Springfield, Massachusetts in 1886.

The Bettmann Archive, Inc.

The start of a bicycle race in 1890, sponsored by the League of American Wheelmen. The stadium and the surface suggest that the riders are using a trotting track.

As far as can be determined, the first person to race against a horse was Lizzie Bayer, in 1880, in Sacramento, California. But it was when Arthur Zimmerman and Willie Windle, two of America's best amateur racers, broke the mile record established by the trotting horse Nancy Hanks, that the contest received most attention.

Some writers saw the race between man and beast in terms other than speed. "The new mile record that was made yesterday by the bicyclist, beating the record for the trotting horse, is a more fruitful, if not a more remarkable, performance than that of Nancy Hanks. There is really no other form of sport that works so directly for the good in so many directions as bicycling. Not only do the wheelmen and wheelwomen themselves get the benefit of an invigorating exercise, but whenever they penetrate they do good. It is to their initiative that the improvement of country roads is due. They have also caused signboards to be erected in the regions, to the great comfort of all travelers, by whatever mode of convenience, and they have also been the means of a very great improvement in mapmaking, so that good maps may now be obtained of districts of which no maps were accessible before the wheel began its peaceful revolution. In truth, the bicyclist, though he may neither look it nor know it, is a very considerable public benefactor."

The Racer and the Thoroughbred

Americans were frequently awed by the spectacular accomplishments of riders such as "Jimmy" Michael, who raised the efficiency of the bicycle to an esthetic level. "The tremendous speed of the little Welsh wheelman, Michael," the *New York Times* reported in 1897, "lends some confirmation to the theory that the combination of light weight and a strong pair of legs ought to produce a fast rider. Michael weighs 100 pounds, and his leg muscles are like steel. He rides easily, but his great speed is made easier by his trick of riding close up to the quartet that 'paces' him. A big machine with four riders necessarily overcomes the resistance of air, and riding at their heels the little racer has something like a vacuum in front of him, and air in swift, eddying, and favorable motion on both sides.

"His 30 miles in 59 minutes and 44 seconds is good railroad

speed; while his feat of making 32 miles, every one of which was ridden in less than two minutes, leaves the trotting horse forever outclassed."

Once the trotter's time was bettered, the racers sought to beat the mile mark of the running horse. John S. Johnson, who boasted of being the fastest rider in the world, eclipsed the thoroughbred's mark in 1894. The following account from *Harpers Weekly* suggests the importance of the occasion.

"The thoroughbred race horse is believed to be the swiftest animal on the globe. So when the king of racers, Salvator, covered a mile on a straight track at Monmouth Park on August 28, 1890, in one minute, thirty-five and one-half seconds—which is still the record—he probably went the distance in less time than it was ever traversed before or since by a living creature of any kind moving unaided over the surface of the earth. Had anyone at that time

Races between horses and cyclists were hotly contested. This 1881 sketch shows the trial of speed between Miss Elsa Von Blumen, on an ordinary, and the trotting mare Hattie R, at Rochester, New York.

predicted that within five years a man on a bicycle would propel
himself over the same distance on a similar or any other track in
faster time than that of the thoroughbred, he would have been
considered something more than a visionary. At that time the
bicyclist was competing with the trotting horse, but that he would
ever equal the runner was not dreamed of even by ultra-en-
thusiasts.

"And yet the undreamed of feat has now been accomplished.
Since the advent of the pneumatic-tired wheel with ball bearings,
records have been falling before the bicycle more rapidly than
before the trotter—until of late, several wheelmen have been going miles below two minutes, leaving the trotter quite out of the
race. But no bicyclist had come within striking distance of the
speed of even an ordinary thoroughbred until of a sudden a
professional racing cyclist, John S. Johnson, the 'Western
Wonder,' took 14 seconds off the bicycle record at a single clip and
eclipsed not only some but all thoroughbreds by riding a mile in
one minute, thirty-five and two-fifths seconds. The feat was accomplished over a straight track at Buffalo, New York, on October 24.
The pacemakers were four men mounted on a quadruplet machine.

"Thus for the first time in world history a man has propelled
himself a mile purely by muscular exertion faster than the muscles
of any other living creature ever carried it over the earth's surface.
As a triumph of human development this achievement is therefore
unique, and worthy of record quite apart from its interest to the
sportsmen."

Man and Machine

Society as a whole looked upon the bicycle as a replacement
for the horse. So it was natural that the early tracks were based on
the horseracing circuit. The first riders were content to race on
grass or dirt tracks. But as the bicycle improved, so did the speeds.
Accordingly, track managers saw the need for banking to keep the
riders from flying off the track at the bends. In time many of the old
dirt tracks were cemented over and given steeper banking.

Other considerations also affected the size, shape, and surface
of bicycle racing tracks. One was the advent of paced racing in the

Bicycle racing was popular in Harrisburg, Pennsylvania at the turn of the century. Shown are cyclers from the Susquehanna Cyclers Club preparing to race along the Susquehanna River.

early 1890s. With the ordinary bicycles the riders were forced to go at top speed from the gun. However, with the coming of the low bicycle, the competitors found that they could take shelter behind their rivals, coming out at the end of the race and sprinting, comparably fresh, to the finish.

This development led to loafing rivals who would be reluctant to go to the front and give shelter to the other racers. So the idea of putting in an outside pacer, who would not be eligible for a prize, was put into practice in 1894. Because of the speeds of the racers, it was soon learned that one pacing tandem was not enough. Each man needed a full army of pacers.

Some rugged individuals used trains to break speed records. The man who undertook the greatest number of train-paced rides was Mile-a-Minute Anderson, who made his last attempt behind a steam train in Chicago on Independence Day, 1898, reaching speeds exceeding 59 miles per hour.

Charles Murphy, champion amateur racer who dreamed of achieving speeds only the railroad flyers could reach, was the first to reach 60 miles per hour on his bike. He insisted that there was no moving object he could not keep pace with if he was shielded from atmospheric resistance. This claim earned him much ridicule, but he continued to plead his case until he was given permission to attempt the ride on a section of the Long Island Railroad.

A plank pathway was laid between the rails near Farmingdale for a distance of almost three miles. After several unsuccessful trial runs, a heavier and speedier engine was assigned to the experiment. Racing along the shifting plankway, peppered by cinders, dust and dirt, Murphy traveled so fast that he actually had to slow down to avoid hitting the train.

Thirty-five years after his successful ride, Murphy recalled his triumph. "Second by second I crept back into view. Whew, what a relief at the signal of the American flag, signifying the finish. The joy in my heart of success and a moment more of suspense. I was riding faster than the train itself, as I was still making up lost ground. Head still over the handlebars, pedaling more fiercely than I ever did before, it seemed like an endless task.

The Bettmann Archive, Inc.

Charles N. "Mile-a-Minute" Murphy riding behind a Long Island Railroad train, June 30, 1899.

"As Sam Booth, the engineer, passed the mile mark he shut off the steam. The locomotive slowed too suddenly; on I came and crashed head-on into the rear of the train. The front wheel recoiled, while the back wheel rebounded and continued to revolve in the air. I pitched forward as a yell of despair went up from the officials on the rear platform. They expected me to be dashed to pieces and sure death. The men on the back of the platform reached out in sheer nervousness and gradually drew me close.

"The pleasure and glory of my long-cherished idea was not to be taken from me by death. I reached forward, grabbed an upright on the rear of the car as Hal Fullerton, then special agent for the railroad, caught me by the arm and pulled both the bicycle and myself up to the platform of the rear car."

American Champions

The first official American champion was George M. Hendee, of Springfield, Massachusetts, who won the title in 1883 in a road race. Since this was perhaps the first contest of record in the country, Hendee became top rider by virtue of winning. Hendee, a tall, graceful champion, earned a reputation as one of the finest ordinary riders in the country. Although Hendee was considered an amateur, in truth he marks the beginning of professionalism in bicycle racing, as he abandoned everything else in life to devote himself to racing. And he was a great success and crowd-pleaser.

Racing was fast becoming a national sport. It was not uncommon for a race in Springfield, Massachusetts, or Peoria, Illinios, to draw crowds as large as 23,000. So popular was the sport that night racing was started in Philadelphia in June, 1884.

Another early American champion from this period was Arthur Augustus Zimmerman, who was never known as anything but "Zimmy" or "Zim" all his racing life. Beginning his racing career on an ordinary, Zimmy afterwards adopted the "Star" bicycle which had an up-and-down action. The "Star" also had the small wheel in the front and the large wheel at the rear, the opposite of the normal high-wheeled machines of the time. The "Star" treadles were so arranged that the rider could have both feet at the top of the stroke, ready for a powerful and fast start.

George M. Hendee, American Amateur Champion, 1883–1885, with his 55-inch ordinary.

Arthur Augustus Zimmerman. "Zimmy" was the first World Sprint Champion, 1893. Note the toe clips and the small chainwheel.

2,300 PRIZES AND UNPARALLELED LIST OF RIDERS WHO HAVE BECOME CHAMPIONS DURING 1892
L. CANTU, CHAMPION OF ITALY.
A. RUSCELLI, CHAMPION DES JUNIORS OF ITALY.
A. GERICKE, CHAMPION OF AUSTRIA
W. FRIEDRICH CHAMPION (LONG DISTANCE OF) AUSTRIA
J.D. CELLIERS CHAMPION OF SOUTH AFRICA
S. LENTON CHAMPION (50 MILES OF) WALES.
AND

A.A. ZIMMERMAN, N.Y.A.C.

Arthur Zimmerman, New York A.C., in 1893. From a "Raleigh" advertising poster. (Amateurs' victories were advertised in those days.)

Zimmy's racing feats were phenomenal and known the racing world over. In 1892, as an amateur, Zimmy won 75 races. Turning professional in 1894, Zimmy went to France, England, Ireland, and Germany, winning more than a hundred races. He was one of the first athletes to "cash in" on his name and fame. Accordingly, there were "Zimmy" shoes, "Zimmy" toe clips, and "Zimmy" clothing.

While still an amateur in 1893, he won the following prizes: 15 bicycles, 15 finger rings, 15 diamonds, 14 medals, 2 cups, 7 studs, 8 watches, 1 city lot, 6 clocks, 4 scarfpins, 9 pieces of silverware, 2 bronzes, 2 wagons, 1 piano, and numerous other valuable prizes.

Zimmy raced extensively in Europe and Australia, winning most of his races. He was lionized wherever he went. He was invited by the governor's wife in Victoria, Australia to demonstrate bicycle riding in the ballroom of the palace. Zimmy drew 27,000 fans at an opening day race in Sydney, Australia, the largest crowd he ever rode for.

In 1896 there were 692 professional track racers and 250 Class B riders. Zimmy stood at the head of these racers. According to a newspaper account of the day, "In many respects Mr. A. A. Zimmerman stands alone, as the greatest racer the world has produced. He has been for several years by common consent the

champion of the world in competitive contests where brain, brawn, and muscle necessarily combine for supremacy. He has proved his title in this country and in Europe."

Women on the Wheel

The entry of women into bicycle racing was greeted with hoots of laughter and derision. However, with the genuine athletic feats of speed and endurance performed by such top-notch riders as Lisette of France, Clara Grace of Scotland, and Frankie Nelson of America, racing for women came to be taken as seriously as the men's branch of the sport. Of course, the early women riders and racers flew in the face of conventional morality, echoed in the words of a Chicago police captain, "I am not an advocate of the use of the bicycle among women, when viewing it from a morality phase. Women of refinement and exquisite moral training addicted to the use of the bicycle are not infrequently thrown among the un-cultivated and degenerate elements of both sexes whose coarse, boisterous, and immoral gestures are heard and seen while speed-ing along our streets and boulevards. Many doubtless escape the contamination, although the contagion may be ever present.

"A large number of our female cyclists wear shorter dresses than the laws of morality and decency permit, thereby inviting the improper conversations and remarks of the depraved and the im-moral. I most certainly consider the adoption of the bicycle by women as detrimental to the advancement of morality."

Most objections to women riders and racers were squashed when fashionable society took up the bicycle. Racing women had some serious backing from some well-known members of their sex. Mrs. Stanley, wife of the explorer, toured extensively, and wrote about her cycling experiences. Fanny Workman, one of the first long-distance female riders, cycled through Africa in 1898.

The racing women took full advantage of the public accep-tance of cycling. They consciously set out to put serious records on the books and to get their racing accepted by the governing bodies. Nonetheless, the world governing body of racing did not officially recognize women's racing until the 1950s.

The greatest woman rider of the period was Lisette (many of the racing women used either a *nom de plume* or their forenames;

it was still not "ladylike" to race). Lisette was discovered by "Choppy" Warbuton, a famous coach, at a farm near Clermont-Ferrand. He took her to Paris where she was soon the top track rider. She then went to England and won hundreds of prizes against the best professional women.

In 1896 women's racing was also going well in America, although curiously, American women preferred the road to the track. Nevertheless, women of the class of Frankie Nelson were very soon dispelling any doubts about their serious athletic ambitions. At age 19 she was USA women's professional champion. Frankie was also invited to France and Germany. In England she raced in several "mixed" Six-Day races. She won the first American Women's "Six" in 1895 at Madison Square Garden and won two more the next year.

Frankie Nelson, a great world-class rider, wasn't blessed with such a "home crowd" as were European women. Interestingly, the champion American women racers of the 1970s, including Sheila Young, Sue Novara, and Mary Jane Reoch, tend to be far better known in Europe than they are in this country.

Many women in the 1890s who were not professional or even amateur racers performed incredible feats on the bicycle. Jane Yatman, who worked for a book firm in New York, cycled 700 miles in 81 hours and 5 minutes. Skyrockets and a large crowd of admirers greeted her as she crossed the finish line in a drenching rainstorm.

To ride multiple centuries (hundreds of miles) became a challenge for a number of women of the Century Road Club and other organizations. Within a month of Jane Yatman's record, Mrs. Jane Lindsay, a Long Island housewife, rode 800 miles in 91 hours and 48 minutes, establishing yet another world record.

No prizes were offered. Lindsay rode over the muddy and slippery country roads of Long Island just to establish a record, to test her own endurance. A newspaper account describes her ride:

"Her impressions of her ride were very vague. At first the country, looking gay and very beautiful in its glorious Autumn tints, afforded some distractions to her. But during the second and third hundred miles, the hardest period of her journey, all the landscape, she declared, appeared black to her. At times she was very dizzy and felt as though she would fall off her wheel. She suffered from severe pains in her wrists and knees, and after the second century it was agony to her to lift her feet. After the four hundredth mile the pain subsided and she suffered most from want of sleep.

"At the conclusion of the ride, after being fed and bathed, Mrs. Lindsay slept uneasily for three hours, when she was made to rise and walk for an hour. Then she slept for two more hours, was aroused again, went for a walk, and retired to bed once more and fell into a sound sleep. Save that deep lines had been furrowed around her mouth and that her eyes were sunken, she appeared little the worse for her journey, and expressed the determination to take the road again to defeat anyone who attempted to break her record. 'I guess they won't try it in a hurry, though,' she added."

The annals of women's racing are filled with accounts of the heroic as well as the bizarre. In 1893 Mrs. A. M. C. Allen of Worcester, Massachusetts was an invalid, hardly able to move about. In 1897 she cycled 21,026 miles, a new record for American women. She was in the saddle 266 days of the year. The *New York Times* reports that "Her longest ride was 153 miles, and in returning home a ferocious dog fastened its teeth to her ankle. She drew a revolver and shot the animal, and then pedaled 16 miles before receiving medical attention."

Even at the turn of the century, society often impeded attempts by women to enter the record books. In 1900 Marguerite Gast, the German rider, attempted to establish a new long distance record for women by riding 5,000 miles within a month. Riding 16 hours and an average of 200 miles a day on Long Island roads, she was approximately halfway to her goal when the District Attorney of Nassau County ordered her to stop. Neighbors complained that the spectacle corrupted their children. The District Attorney remarked, "I consider it improper, immoral, and illegal to make such an exhibition on the public highway."

If Americans of the late-nineteenth and early-twentieth centuries had a love affair with speed, they also had a love affair with distance. Thousand-mile and cross-country races were not uncommon. Marguerite Gast herself established many long-distance road records, none of which the male-dominated national body would recognize. It is on record that Gast sometimes beat men at the really long races, up to a thousand miles.

First Black Champion

In many respects the bicycle was the "great leveler," an instrument of social equality. It gave many women mobility and a certain freedom. It gave the countryside to all who desired it. When the best minds were applied to bicycle construction and the manufacturing of the machine became big business, participation in the sport grew. Notably, the professional ranks flourished. Americans were hungry for all sorts of competition involving the bicycle. Not surprisingly, men and women were attracted to racing as a livelihood. Promoters established a racing circuit that took in Manhattan Beach, New York; Peoria, Illinois; Indianapolis, Indiana; and Cape Girardeau, Missouri.

Because of the intense participation at the high school, college, and community levels, there was always a good supply of capable amateur riders moving into the professional ranks. What is true of football, basketball, and baseball today was true of cycling less than a hundred years ago: bicycle racing was a real inducement to riders who desired to earn a living in the most popular, competitive, and demanding spectator sport that existed in America. For every rich man's son who was successful, there is a milkman's son or daughter who became a champion of the wheel.

One of the most compelling stories to come out of the period is that of Marshall W. "Major" Taylor, who is generally considered the first black world's champion. Although there were many incidents of blacks being barred from riding in particular races, bike racing in general never suffered from the color bar. Nonetheless, a black rider had to overcome numerous obstacles on the circuit. We had occasion to read some of Major Taylor's letters, written to his wife in early 1900s. In Paris at the time, Taylor revealed the extreme human difficulty of professional racing. His was a Spartan existence. He was spurred on by his intense commitment to his family, his people, and his profession. Although he wanted to compete against the world's finest racers, his deep loneliness drove him near to despair.

"Major" Taylor, World Professional Sprint Champion, 1899. Considered by many to be the fastest sprinter ever to ride, he is fondly remembered in Europe and largely forgotten in America.
Major Taylor and Frank Kramer at the start of a Match race, circa 1900.

Ironically, Major Taylor is far better known in France and other parts of Europe than in his own country. It is not uncommon for a modern-day Frenchman to remark about a young rider: "He rides like Major Taylor." Considering Taylor's lightning speed, his unique position on the bike, and his ability to come from behind in a track race and outmaneuver and outsprint his opponents, it is not surprising that his name is invoked to describe the best young racers of today.

There were many black racers in America during this period. As in the rest of society, however, their activities often were separate from those of the white riders. All-black touring clubs existed in many parts of the country, particularly cities such as New York, Indianapolis, and Chicago. On most occasions, however, a black racer could enter a sanctioned race if he chose.

Major Taylor's early efforts to race at the Capital City Race Track in Indianapolis were not without incident. After he had done well in road races in Peoria and Indianapolis, Taylor's friends secretly arranged for him to beat the existing mile record established by Walter, one of the greatest sprinters of the day. Taylor lowered the mark by seven seconds and was banished from all Indianapolis tracks.

From that time his rise was meteoric. With help from Louis D. Munger, a bicycle manufacturer, and encouragement from champion riders such as Zimmy and Willie Windle, Taylor improved rapidly. He trained with the high school and college athletes in Indianapolis to help improve his form.

Moving to Worchester, Massachusetts, he became a professional in 1896, winning a half-mile race at Madison Square Garden against some of the best professionals in the country. Two years later he won the one-mile World Sprint title in Montreal. But perhaps the most thrilling days of Taylor's racing career were during his victories in Europe and Australia.

In 1901 he beat Edmond Jacquelin and Thorwald Elleggarde, champions of France and Denmark respectively. Taylor provides an account of his race with the French hero in his autobiography, *The Fastest Bicycle Rider in the World*, published in 1928.

"Upwards of thirty thousand eager, impatient bicycle race enthusiasts greeted Jacquelin and I with a storm of applause as we came out to face the starter. The Frenchman had his same arrogant smile as he mounted his wheel. As we rode slowly from the tape in the first heat there was great cheering. After some maneuvering Jacquelin and I tried to force each other into the lead. In so doing both of us came to a dead stop. We were practically side by side, Jacquelin being slightly ahead. Balancing a few moments, I backed slowly half a revolution of my crank until I brought myself directly behind Jacquelin. That's just where I wanted to be. The grandstands were now in a frenzy. Realizing that I had outmaneuvered him on this score, Jacquelin laughed outright and moved off in the lead prepared for business.

"I was so satisfied that I could bring him into camp on this occasion that I again allowed him to ride his own pace. I played right into his hands and actually permitted him to start his famous jump from his favorite distance, about 250 yards from the tape. However, I was very careful to jump at the same instant and the sprint down the long straight stretch must have been magnificent.

Jacquelin was four lengths behind when I dashed across the tape.
The applause was deafening."

It was quite common for Taylor's opponents to force him into a
"pocket," from where they could control his final sprint. Originally
Major Taylor would stay behind the rest of the field, starting his
sprint from the rear of the field and exposing himself to rough riding tactics. Later, he realized his best defense would be to shoot
into the lead during the last lap of a race and begin his sprint from
the front of the pack. This tactic proved indispensable during his
illustrious 16-year career.

Despite an occasional problem with the National Cycling
Association and a few of the professional riders, Taylor rode and
was enthusiastically received throughout the country. Having
beaten most of the greats on the tracks of America, Europe, and
Australia, Major Taylor retired in 1910, returning to the Newark
velodrome to win an old-timers' race in 1917. He had earned the
title of the "fastest bicycle rider in the world." He seemed to relish
one nickname in particular, that of the "black Zimmerman."

For all the successes Major Taylor experienced during his final
years in racing, especially those spent in Europe, he was a lonely
man, apart from his family, sensing that he was losing his form. His
anguish and loneliness are revealed in this poignant letter to his
wife, in which he explains that the French promoter, Coquelle,
cannot offer him a good contract for the coming year:

"Well dearie, I had a talk with Coquelle about next season,
and it is all off. He did not tell me outright that he could not engage
me, but told me openly that he could not give me what I asked for
and of course I could not come over for what he offered me, so like
that I may try riding on the other side next year, though I should
hate to get mixed up with those dirty sandbaggers anymore. You
see, dearie, Coquelle has no money himself, and he can not
guarantee me a dollar. He can only arrange races equivalent to
whatever price he agrees to pay me, for my end of it, then in case I
fail to make good in my races, then my price varies just according
to my winnings, etc. So that the way I rode this season my price
dropped about 50 percent in most of my races. It was not his fault
that I did not ride any better, in fact he did everything for me he
could possibly do to get me to ride well.

"Now after the terrible experience of this season I am not at all grieved because I am not coming over again next year, but quite to the contrary I am indeed pleased. As I told you several times before dearie, I am full up with this business, and have been for a long time, and this season's work just put the finishing touches on it. I regret very much now that I ever came back again, because if I had finished last year, you see how nice it would have been for you and little Sydney to have been with me on my last *successful* racing season, and we could have finished by trimming them all, and on top, etc. One thing that I *am* pleased for dearie, and that is that you and Sydney were not here to see everybody trimming me this year, so perhaps it is just as well that you did not come.

"Well at any rate I can say that I had a good, honest, faithful *try*, and did the very *best* I could *every* time, and the fault was surely not mine. There is one possible solution to why I could do no better under the circumstances, and this I have told you many times. I was thinking seriously about having you and Sydney come over alone, and in fact I had spoken for a small house, I thought if Coquelle wanted me for next season it would be just as well if I remained on this side all winter and keep in shape by racing on the indoor track this winter, but the outlook for a new indoor track is very unfavorable just at this time. As far as I can learn it will not be finished until next spring, if then, they have not even begun to work on it as yet, so that is all off.

"Oh well, if I can finish up these last two races without a fall and get home safely, etc., I will be most thankful indeed, and I will be even still more grateful if I can find you and dear little Sydney both well, and everything alright otherwise. I hope by the way dearie that you are not entertaining too much, and that you are trying to save as much money as you possibly can, because as I told you, I have not done too well this time, and I will have lots of things to do when I come home that will probably take about all we can scrape up, so be as careful as you can dearie. I know in fact that you are careful, but you know just what I mean, don't you, don't deprive yourself or Sydney of anything (within the bounds of reason), that will make you comfortable or happy, do your very best, it is only for a few weeks longer, and then I will be there to look out for both of my girls, just nine days after today and I shall have finished one of the most severe tests of my life.

"Say dearie, how anxiously I am counting every minute of the time that remains, just as I imagine one in jail or prison must feel after doing about five years of hard labor. Each month that I have put in over here seems like a year to me, but thank God it will soon be over with, and then I can return to you dearie, well and strong, just as I left you, please God. So cheer up, be in good trim for me, dearie, because I have been to see two or three prize fights over here and I have learned a lot of new hooks, jabs etc."

Indoor Racing

During Taylor's racing career there were well over 100 gravel, dirt, cinder, cement, and wood tracks in America. The vast upsurge in the building of modern wooden velodromes soon put the United States at the top of the ladder in international racing. With the great popularity of outdoor racing, promoters soon constructed a racing circuit of indoor velodromes. The unique style of racing engineered by indoor velodromes took the public fancy. The riders also saw indoor racing as a new and exciting experience. According to an article written for a Boston newspaper by Nat Butler, champion turn-of-the-century rider, "Indoor bicycle racing is a distinct branch of the sport. To the eye of the spectator it resembles the contest on wheels outdoors. The same riders compete, apparently the same methods are pursued, and when the last jump commences the best man wins. But this is not so, strictly speaking.

Courtesy of Dick Swann

Bicycle track, Waltham, Massachusetts, 1896.

As in racing on outdoor tracks, the ability to unwind the pedals fast is an essential requirement for indoor work. Still more necessary, though, is the nerve, fearlessness, or recklessness as some might term it, which impels a rider to shoot around a steep track to what seems almost instantaneous death.

"One who has not ridden at a swift gait on a short, highly banked indoor track cannot imagine the sensation of it. As you start off along the straightaway your wheel is scarcely in motion before you are hill climbing. Up the bank you go, and just as you accustom yourself to the idea of riding up an incline your wheel swerves and down the other side of the bank you drop in a harassing manner. Then around the undulating oval you fly, going faster and faster as you get into full stride.

"After the second lap it is bewildering. One moment you go straight ahead, the next you are swinging around dizzily in a manner akin to riding along the side of a wall. To me the excitement and danger of it all, are fascinating. Probably that's why I ride so much better indoors than out. I like the dazzling lights and the echoing of the cheers and shouts. The tumult goads me on until I fear nothing.

"Crouched low on my wheel, with hands firmly gripping the bars, I make every thrust of the pedals whirl me around faster. By the time the clanging bell and the frantic yells of the crowd announce the last lap, I am just as wild as the most demonstrative onlooker. I know nothing but the spice of victory. I go around like a wooden animal in a carnival. My body swings in unison with my faithful steed. As I near the upward incline my torso and head bend toward the inside, and when I am at the summit of the rise my wheel and myself are at right-angles to the track. Instinctively my body swings back again as I dive down the bank toward the straight."

Butler's exciting description of an indoor race remains as a classic as it explains what drove the early American riders to attempt such feats and why they captured the fancy of so many people.

America was to close out the nineteenth century with high interest in the bicycle. Although it was no longer as popular as it once was among the upper strata of society, it was firmly

A bicycle racer at a cement track, 1900.

entrenched in the American sports, recreation, and fitness scene. The New York social set was beginning to forsake the bicycle for the car, but the shopboys, newspaper carriers, carpenters, and other trademen continued to use the bicycle. Racing was a highly popular spectator sport. It was not uncommon to see 20,000 spectators at a race, while across the street, 2,500 attended a baseball game.

The League of American Wheelmen, the official cycling organization, had 100,000 members. Bicycle racing had infiltrated the country, and tracks could be found in some of the most unlikely places: Chillicothe, Ohio; Mahanoy City, Pennsylvania; Marshall, Michigan, and dozens of other places.

Bike racing, an intricate part of family and community entertainment, was as much a part of county fairs and holidays as the flag ceremonies. Colleges and high schools regularly fielded teams.

Professional racers were national and international heroes. America was the center for track sport. Babe Ruth will never be as well-known in Europe as the American track heroes of the period.

CHAPTER TWO

The Six-Day

JAMES C. MC CULLAGH

THE American bike riders of the late 1890s and early 1900s spearheaded a sporting invasion of Europe. In fact, there was an American sporting colony in Paris, which included Bobby Walthour, Sr., Nat Butler, and Frank Kramer, all National and World champions. Walthour, the first of three racing members of his family, was probably the most popular and most loved American athlete overseas. An English newspaper described him in 1904 as the "most popular athlete in history." Not surprisingly, he was followed around Paris and Berlin by admiring crowds whenever he left his hotel room.

American World Champions

According to Jimmy Walthour, Bobby's nephew and a champion rider in the 1920s and 1930s, "Bobby left his mark on cycling as very few men have done, with the exception of Eddie Merckx (currently considered the finest rider in the world). He was perhaps the greatest all-around rider of all times. He won Six-Day races in New York when they were really tough. He cleaned up everything in America, then went to Europe.

"He gained such a reputation that he could have been governor of Georgia. The name was that famous. He was a hero. When he came to New York for a Six-Day, the Vanderbilts and the Goulds would have a box for the week and if he wasn't in the race, they would cancel out.

"He was so well-known that when he eloped with the belle of Atlanta, a songwriter based 'A Bicycle Built for Two' on his elopement."

Known as the "Dixie Flyer" at home, Bobby Walthour, Sr., won hundreds of track races in Germany, England, and France. Perhaps his greatest ride was the 1909 World Paced Championship in Denmark.

He was hampered by a pacing machine that squirted oil from a broken pipe all over him. Nonetheless, even with his body and his bicycle covered with oil, he managed to finish the race.

In addition to international heroes such as Walthour, America also had racing champions who spent most of their racing careers at home. One such star is Frank L. Kramer, undoubtedly the king of track racing in America. A bike shop owner in Irvington, New Jersey told this writer that going to see Frank Kramer race "was like going to see the President."

While it might seem strange to present-day Americans that bicycle racing and racers could command so much interest and respect, it was not at all strange to Jimmy Walthour. He remarked that "people have to understand that racing was something a young boy or girl would grow up with. Standing in the bleachers with 18,000 spectators, watching the man and his machine move through the smallest opening in a crowd of racers, was a real thrill. I loved it as a boy. The hair went up on my arms and tears came to my eyes. I wanted then and there to be a bike racer. Kids in my day identified as closely with Bobby Walthour, Sr., and Frank Kramer as the kids today identify with Joe Namath. No one who knew anything about bike racing would conceive of going to a baseball game if a bike race was scheduled. I can remember plenty of times in New York that, if you didn't get to the track early enough, you wouldn't get a seat."

One of the reasons racing continued its popularity through the first two decades of the new century was Frank Kramer. In the opinions of the sports writers of his day, he was to racing what Babe Ruth and Jack Dempsey were to their sports. He was professional Sprint champion in America for 18 years, 16 of them consecutively. Ty Cobb never held the batting crown for 16 straight years;

no fighter ever remained undefeated for that amount of time. Kramer was one of a kind.

As was true of many cyclists of the day, Kramer took to cycling for health reasons. At the age of 10, he contracted tuberculosis. His father give him a bicycle, and almost immediately his health began to improve. As signs of the disease began to disappear, Kramer entered some amateur races in New Jersey. His rapid progress,

Courtesy of "Pop" Brennan Bike Shop

Frank Kramer, professional American Sprint champion for 18 years, remains as one of the country's greatest athletes.

aided by his father's enthusiastic training, led Kramer to his first national championship when he was 18. In 1900 he turned professional and shook the cycling establishment by taking second place to Major Taylor in the Professional Sprint Championship. He remained professional Sprint champion during this country's most competitive years. He also won the World Professional Sprint Championship in 1912.

Kramer's Spartan lifestyle has become something of a legend. He was noted for his iron discipline, for his reluctance to burn the candle at both ends. He believed in eating as little as possible. For 25 years he went to bed at 9:00 P.M., except when he raced. He had been known to walk out of a banquet in order to get his rest. He never smoked or drank until after his retirement. He lived entirely for racing.

Willie Ratner, famous Newark sportswriter, remarked that watching "Kramer ride was like watching Bobby Jones play golf, Jack Dempsey in action, or Babe Ruth at bat. They all had the thing called 'class' which comes naturally to some athletes, but which others couldn't develop in a thousand years. A man must be born with it and Kramer sure was for he was a star from the first to the last day that he straddled his bike."

Courtesy of "Pop" Brennan Bike Shop

Kramer ready for Match Sprint with French idol Friol in Paris, France, circa 1912.

Kramer and French idol Gabriel Poulain at a Paris velodrome, circa 1912.

By virtue of his fine records abroad (in 1905 he won 22 of 25 races), he gained a large following in Europe. Americans who traveled to Europe during this period were frequently queried as to his health. Above all, however, Kramer was a gentleman and an American. Commenting on his victory in a prestigious French race, Kramer remarked: "The race that gave me the biggest thrill was in 1912 in Paris, when I won the Grand Prix and heard America's national anthem 'The Star-Spangled Banner,' played as I made the tour of honor around the saucer. It certainly felt great to hear those strains on foreign land." He was in the opinion of Alf Goullet, a great racer who competed against Kramer, the "greatest athlete ever."

On July 26, 1922, at the age of 42, Kramer retired. Some fans cried when the announcement was made. To show the 20,000 Newark fans his appreciation for their support, Kramer proceeded to break the lap record at the track. "Even without this final flourish," a newspaper reported, "Kramer's record is one of the most marvelous in athletic history."

Frank Kramer prepares for a Match Sprint against Edmond Jacquelin, Champion of France.

Behind the Motors

In Kramer's hometown of Newark and at outdoor tracks in Boston, New York, Hartford, Providence, and Worchester, velodrome racing remained a big draw into the 1920s. A rider who followed the circuit could expect to ride seven days a week, racing in front of 40,000 people. A typical racer could compete at the New York Velodrome on Tuesday, Friday, and Sunday night, and at the Newark Velodrome on Wednesday, Thursday, and Sunday afternoon. Most of the professional riders on the circuit were married with children. And according to Jimmy Walthour, "everyone made a decent living."

During the first decades of the twentieth century, neither the cyclists nor the fans lost interest in speed on the track. It must be remembered that bike racing in this period took place against the backdrop of a society which was becoming steadily mechanized. The center of interest, at least for the lay public, shifted from the bicycle to the internal combustion engine. Many in the bike business went into the automotive industry. Henry Ford, a friend of

G. Schoefield being paced by the pacing team of the famous Kings County Wheelmen, at Manhattan Beach cement track, 1897.

First Race, 8:20 P. M. Sharp.

Races Friday Night, Aug. 2
1899.
TEN RACES AT THE COLOSSEUM.

Including the Great Motor Paced Match Race, 5-mile heats, best 2 in 3, between Nat.
Butler, of Boston, Colosseum King Champion, and Jimmie Bowler, of Chicago, holder
of the 1-2 mile World's Record. Purse $500, including side bet of $100.

Admission: Arena, 25 cents;   Grand Stand, 50 cents.

An 1899 motor used to pace Nat Butler. The bike is driven by both pedal and motor power.

Motor pacing in the early part of the twentieth century. Tandem racing never completely fell out of popularity. Here is Joyce Dean racing in London in 1946 behind a tandem.

Bobby Walthour Jr. (left) and Alf Goullet await the start of a race in Madison Square Garden.

Frank Kramer, is fondly remembered by Alf Goullet as one of the best bicycle mechanics around.

By 1912 the motorcycle had become the rage, and tracks for racing the machine were constructed in many parts of the country. There was a motorcycle track right across the street from the velodrome in Newark. Because of the rash of accidents, cities passed ordinances outlawing motorcycle competition. With that ruling the velodromes also lost motor-paced racing.

Racers in the 1890s had discovered a simple law of physics: if they had a shield against atmospheric pressure, they could go faster. Although the pacing machines originally were used to help the rider break speed records, after Welsh champion Jimmy Michael introduced paced racing to a tumultuous crowd of 30,000 at Manhattan Beach, New York the event became a regular velodrome feature.

In the beginning the style of pacing used was tandems, triplets, and quadricycles, manned by two, three, and four riders, respectively. W. J. Young, trainer of five racing champions, remarked that "The changing of the tired pacemakers by relays of fresh men was a sight to thrill one." The introduction of the gasoline engine all but did away with the changing of pace and the employing of 30 or 40 pacemakers by each contestant. With the advent of the motor bike, the hour record tumbled from 32 to 47 miles an hour within a single year.

To accommodate these new speeds new tracks with banking as high as 45 degrees were constructed. The smaller tracks led to greater speeds and to more accidents. In fact, accidents happened at nearly every race in the early years of motor pacing. The tires, holding 80 pounds of pressure and quickly worn on the track, were always liable to burst. One eyewitness to late nineteenth century motor-pacing said that "the risk these men take in following the motors is awful, for they can never fall back more than a few inches from the pacemaker. To the spectator it looks as though they were held by a string.

"Should anything happen to the machine it is almost an impossibility for the rider to turn out or slow down quickly enough, and the result—a bad smashup. There have been some cases in which a motor, after falling to the track and throwing the pacemaker, the power still being on, has kept the chain and wheels still revolving at terrific speed, grinding and splintering the track and injuring anyone who might fall under or on the sputtering demon."

The toll taken of pace followers was awesome. Johnny Nelson, Archie McEachern, Harry Elkes, and Jimmy Michael, are just a few of the American and World champions to be killed as a result of following the motor.

Racing in Atlanta in 1903, Bobby Walthour, Sr. was traveling at a tremendous speed behind the motor, threatening to break all existing speeds. Then his tire burst and he was thrown heavily against a post. So badly was he injured that the attending physician gave him no chance of surviving. When he began to recover, the doctor said he would never ride again. But he did, and went on to win the World championship.

"Pace followers," commented W. J. Young, "toy with death every time they ride. It takes a man with nerves of steel to climb back to his wheel after so miraculous an escape, but they still do it and as the craze for speed will aways be one of the desires of the racing spectators, so will be the greater danger they face."

Before long, however, helmets were made mandatory for the pace followers and engine size of the motors was reduced, limiting speeds to 45 to 55 miles an hour. Outlawed for a few years with the motorcycle, motor pacing returned to the racing card in the early 1920s. For the next two decades it was a central feature of velodrome racing, especially in Newark, New Jersey, which was fast becoming a mecca for track sport.

Since the roads were not very hospitable at this time to the cyclist, he was "driven" to the tracks where there was a balanced program of amateur and professional racing. Big city spectators, reflecting the complex social and ethnic makeup of the country, flocked to see idols such as Letourneur, Georgetti, and Debaets as well as a host of American favorites. The spectators, in some respects, were like the football or baseball fans of today. Although they probably did not engage in any form of cycling themselves, they knew the sport, the participants, and the tactics. According to champion Six-Day rider Alf Goullet of Newark, the "fans knew more about bicycle racing than half the guys that were racing. They knew every move. The crowd could tell when a rider was loafing."

Spectators would give a rider hell if he didn't stay up with the pacer. They were paying 25 cents to get in to the races and they wanted to get their money worth."

"The fans," Goullet added, "had a special relationship to the racers. The kids used to collect cards with the pictures of cycling stars on them. They would trade them as a kid today might trade baseball or football cards. The kids would follow a star. One of the most popular riders of the day was Jackie Clarke. The kids were mad about him. They would follow him all over the neighborhood. He was like a Namath, a Palmer, a Nicklaus."

As late as 1933 the Nutley Velodrome in New Jersey drew 297,000 spectators for 35 scheduled events. One of the reasons for such a good drawing was motor pacing, sometimes referred to as middle-distance racing, since the race was 10 and 25 miles, although distance of 50 or 100 miles were not uncommon.

The motor-paced races were the center of interest because the speed was great and the distance was long. The race represented a union of sometimes five men and machines and a steeply banked, tight oval. The possibility of an accident was ever-present, as was

Courtesy of "Pop" Brennan Bike Shop

Left to right: Champion riders: Fogle, Kramer, Goullet, and Rutt at the Newark velodrome, 1914.

the chance of a record ride. The pacers themselves earned the reputation as daredevils since they would perform seemingly impossible maneuvers to help their men win.

On the back of the motorcycle is a revolving bar, which is strictly a safety device. The secret of following the motor is for the racer to stay as close as possible to the pacer without touching the bar, which would probably cause the rider to lose his pace. If he would bounce back from the pacer, it would be much harder for him to catch up again.

The system of communication between the racer and pacer was strictly an oral one. The pacemakers had ear guards, covered in front but open at the back, making it possible for the men to catch every command from the rider. There was really no way that the pacemaker could tell if he was losing the man behind except by the roar of the crowd. Understandably, a 100-mile race behind a flying machine is a most strenuous sport. A newspaper reporter, observing the champion Letourneur after the long race, remarked that the Frenchman "found his legs buckling under him, nor could the strains of the French national anthem raise him until he had

Courtesy of Dick Swann

Typical pace follower of the boom days at the Vélodrôme d'Hiver, Paris, in the late 1920s.

had a five-minute rest." And the same rider found that he had to tape his hands to prevent the vibrations of the track from putting them to sleep.

The Six-Day

The 1920s were notable times for the expansion of the popularity of Six-Day races. The very first Six-Day races were conducted in halls in the north of England in the 1870s. The races were promoted by tavern owners or local bookmakers. The bikes were ordinaries, the riders wore jockey costumes, and the tracks were flat boards. They were actually the first portable tracks, 10 to 11 laps a mile, and were taken up and moved to new locations much as the circus big top is moved today.

The craze in America at the time was roller skating and managers were looking for something to run as a side attraction. Therefore, bicycle riders on ordinaries were hired to ride from two to eight hours a day, on the same track with the skaters, but on the outside. Before long, promoters discovered that both riders and skaters could take the turns more quickly on a raised or banked track. When the popularity of the bicycle increased, spectators and racers wanted longer and harder races.

The first Six-Day of any note was run in New York in 1889. There were 14 contestants riding safety bikes for 120 hours. Any rider could get off his bike and rest, although it was a certainty that his rivals would take advantage of his absence. So the race became a contest of who could stay on his machine the longest and pedal the most miles. "Plugger" Bill Martin won the first race with 1,400 miles to his credit.

Opposition, however, grew quickly to what was considered an inhuman sport. Newspapers ran lurid accounts of racers hallucinating during a contest in 1896. Tales of doped riders and blood-soaked bandages resulted in a law which restricted riders to 12 hours a day, resulting in the inauguration of the team race which is still popular.

"It is a fine thing," reported a *New York Times* article in 1897, "to demonstrate that a man astride two wheels can, in a Six-Day race, distance a hound, a horse, or a locomotive. It confirms the assumption, no longer much contested, that the human animal is

Courtesy of "Pop" Brennan Bike Shop

The start of a Six-Day bicycle race, Madison Square Garden, 1906.

Courtesy of "Pop" Brennan Bike Shop

Beginning of a Six-Day in Madison Square Garden.

superior to the other animals. But this undisputed thing is being said in too solemn and painful a way at Madison Square Garden.

"An athletic contest in which the participants 'go queer' in their heads, and strain their powers until their faces become hideous with the tortures that rack them, is not sport, it is brutality. It appears from the reports of this singular performance that some of the bicycle riders have actually become temporarily insane during the contest, while all of them are sore, cross, and distorted. Permanent injury is likely to result from the attempt to perform any task that is beyond the limits of what a man can undergo and make up for in one night's sleep. Days and weeks of recuperation will be needed to put the Garden racers in condition, and it is likely that some of them will never recover from the strain.

"The knowledge that a man can propel himself 1,769 miles in 110 ½ hours is purchased too dearly when it costs the reason and the physical well-being of the person who imparts it."

For all the inflated newspaper stories, the Six-Day became an American institution for the next 30 years. Although dozens of cities in the country hosted the race, the Six-Day had the most appeal in New York and Chicago. Jimmy Walthour recalls that the Six-Day was "a big event in the cities, a showstopper. The actor Jim Barton used to close down his performance for the race. Bing Crosby often paid the bills for an injured rider. Al Capone frequently attended the Chicago race. And Babe Ruth never missed a Six-Day if he was in town."

The modern Six-Day which evolved at the turn of the century was more than a flashy, competitive spectator sport involving a dozen two-man teams. It was a week-long demonstration before hundreds of thousands of fans of keen racing tactics and skillful bike handling. It was a rich close-order drill by experts on highly sensitive machines. It was an addiction for both the rider and spectator. It was something that mesmerized Will Rogers and the average fan alike.

During the 1920s and 1930s the two riders, who could alternate on the track as they wished, rode approximately 140 hours, starting at 9:00 P.M. Sunday night and finishing at midnight the next Saturday. The object of the race was for one team to steal a lap on the rest of the pack. Points were also given for winners of sprints. But, as noted by Kyle Crichton in a 1935 issue of *Colliers*, "The jams are the essence of the business. The riders will be going along at a good steady pace when one of them will suddenly dart out from the pack and pick up half a lap before the others are aware of what is happening.

"Instantly, the arena is a bedlam. Down in the middle of the oval, the infield, the relief riders begin tumbling out of their bunks and on their wheels. The men on the saucer are going now at whirlwind speed, sticking close to the curves or riding high on the rim and swooping down at the turns, cutting through openings so narrow the spectators can't even see them. The relief teams start on the flat, picking them up on the fly and touching them off like runners passing the baton in a relay race. All this time the team in front is striving desperately to lap the field and the pursuers are pedaling their heads off to bring them back into the pack.

Jimmy Walthour and Al Crossley, winners of a Six-Day in 1936.

"The jam may end with the lap being won or may be followed by another theft attempt by a smart rider who utilizes the letdown from one jam to start another. Or it may be stopped by a crash. In the jams the riders are making flying pickups and hitting the turns on high. One swerve, a bump, or a failure to crowd through an opening that suddenly closes will bring the pack down in a heap of tangled wheels and broken bones."

The Six-Day required that one member of the team be on the track at all times, and it was the team with the highest mileage that won. If a number of teams were tied, which could be the case, the winner was determined by "sprints" which occurred at four or five stated intervals during the afternoon and evening.

Alf Goullet, who reputedly received $1,000 a day for a Six-Day, wrote in 1926 that the race "is the most grueling contest in athletics because of its sheer monotony. If we weren't mercifully so built that we quickly forget our sufferings, I don't believe there is a man in the world who would ride in more than one. It takes toll of every muscle in the body, of the stomach, of the heart, and while it is being ridden, the mind. In the past 15 years I have ridden in 24 and the only way I can think of describing the riding is as one infernal grind."

Yet Goullet remembers today the thrill of the Six-Day, the theatre and nightclub crowds that cheered him to victory at Madison Square Garden, and the fans who would scream themselves hoarse trying to get the riders to jam.

W. J. "Torchy" Pedem, with his red hair and six-foot three-inch, 220-pound frame, was one of the most loved and feared of the Six-Day riders in the 1930s. He fondly recalls when the Six-Day was the heart of the winter sports calendar, when money, glamour, and high competition were synonymous with the bike game. He remembers driving up to the massive Chicago Stadium in November, 1930 and being awed by the steeply banked indoor track constructed by 100 carpenters. He has never forgotten the scent of western fir and Georgia pine, used to build the track. He can still recall his entrance into the cavernous Chicago Stadium were he was to undergo for the first time the arduous test of six days of racing, 20 hours a day. Fifty years later he remembers the thrill of racing against Alf Letourneur, Pietro Linari, Franco

Georgetti, and other international stars and the anguish of being dropped from the competition on the final night of racing. For Pedem, the Six-Day was the ultimate in board track combat and spectator appeal.

Over the years the Six-Day format has changed considerably. From the earlier racing program, with an emphasis on endurance, has evolved a more formalized race with much of the content determined in advance. According to Jack Simes, champion sprinter and Six-Day rider, the "actual length of the race varies from country to country, with Germany generally having the toughest schedule. In the modern Six-Day the speeds are much faster and, for that reason, I think the race is far more spectacular than it was years ago.

Robert F. George

Sprint won by Willy DeBosscher, Belgium, during a Six-Day in Los Angeles, California, 1973.

"At most tracks today there is a set program. The racer knows when the sprints are coming, when the chase is on, and when other events are going to occur. All the events are coordinated with some form of entertainment, such as singers and comedians, making the race package a truly memorable one.

"The race might progress something like this. The Six-Day begins at 8:00 P.M. with a series of five sprints which would be split between the two-man teams. I might take three sprints and my partner two. After the sprint, there will likely be a chase or a jam for 20 minutes. Later in the evening there might be a race behind the small motors.

"Yet this doesn't mean a rider can't, as in the old days, try to steal a lap apart from the regular program. I have seen and been a part of some tremendous chases when there were few people in attendance at the track. In Montreal a couple of years ago, one of the riders started jamming about 12:30 P.M. and continued the pace for two hours. That's close to 50 miles an hour for two solid hours. I once saw a team that was 39 laps behind the rest of the field and that started jamming at 3:00 in the morning, stealing back 13 laps. So there is still a good bit of the unpredictability commonly associated with the older Six-Days.

"For me, the Six-Day is the ultimate in cycle sport. The body is operating at a maximum level, the challenge is formidable. You are on display in front of fans who know the sport. The race demands bike handling, speed, endurance. Completing the race is like climbing a big mountain.

"There's something eerie and mystical about the race, at least as far as the public is concerned. The spectator enters the stadium and the first thing he hears is the rumbling of the boards. When he looks at the steeply banked track he wonders how on earth anyone can stay up on such an incline. And to witness a chase is incomprehensible to most.

"So the emphasis today is on the spectacle, the entertainment. We might ride only 12 hours a day, but we are still out to win, to make the race a thing of beauty. I think Americans are being deprived of a great sport. I remember watching a Six-Day in New York in 1961. In front of me was a father with his 17-year-old son. The boy was complaining about the race and the racing: he had no

Robert F. George

The jam is on. Eddy Demedts prepares to "sling" his partner Willy DeBosscher during a Six-Day in Detroit in 1973.

Robert F. George

Jack Simes gives John Vande Velde a "hand sling" during a Six-Day in Los Angeles in 1974.

Robert F. George

Six-Day Track, Montreal, Canada (1973).

interest in it. Then the real racing started with cyclists moving at
50 miles an hour and darting in and out of prohibitive space. And
then the boy went crazy. He was screaming and yelling and
thought it was the greatest thing he had ever seen."

The irony is that most Americans today are not aware that at
one time the Six-Day, motor pacing, and other road and track
events constituted high sport and entertainment in this country.
Perhaps the fault was with the sport itself for becoming too specialized, too distant from the recreational needs of the fans.
Whatever the reason, by the late 1930s bike racing as a spectator
sport was finished in this country. Jimmy Walthour recalls an account by Jack Dempsey, the boxer, concerning a Six-Day in the
mid-1930s.

"Dempsey was a real bike fan. Actually, he rode in road races
in Salt Lake City before he went on to such a successful career in
boxing. He was a regular spectator at a Six-Day. I'll never forget
how disappointed he was after witnessing a race in Chicago. What
really upset him was the amateurish handling of the race—no real
promotion, no real publicity. They were actually giving out pencil
sets for the winners of sprints."

Norman Hill, one of America's finest racers in the 1930s.

Roger Young and Paul Deem after winning the first Team Race or Madison held at the Trexlertown, Pennsylvania velodrome.

Jack Dempsey's story can be considered symbolic of the general decline of interest in the bicycle during this period. The real tragedy was that a whole generation grew up without even owning or riding bicycles. This fact, coupled with the destruction of most of the existing velodromes in the country, meant a further decline of the sport.

Fortunately, the Amateur Bicycle League of America (now the United States Cycling Federation) kept the amateur sport alive on the road and at a limited number of tracks. In 1949 Jack Heid of the Century Road Club of America gained third place in the World Amateur Sprint Championship, leading the renaissance. More recently, Jack Simes, Audrey McElmury, Sheila Young, Mary Jane Reoch, and Sue Novara have earned medals for America.

Equally important is the fact that the bicycle is once again receiving serious attention as a vehicle for transportation and health. While it is doubtful that people will ever take to the bike as their forefathers did in the 1890s, it seems very likely that the bicycle will return as an important feature in American life. It also seems likely that the more serious cyclists that exist, the more interest there will be in quality racing. Indications are that Americans are turning to bike racing as a spectator sport. No wonder. America has some of the most promising racers in the world.

CHAPTER THREE

The Spectator, the Rider, and the Race

DAVE CHAUNER

THE narrow, winding road up to the ski station of Pra Loup high in the French Alps sees little traffic during the lazy summer months. A few tourists and vacationers use it on their way to summer homes or to get to the bigger resorts beyond but, for the most part, that steep, twisting band of asphalt is just another quiet Alpine byway.

On July 13, 1975, all that changed. The innocuous road to Pra Loup became a hysterical arena, center stage for one of the most emotional athletic dramas ever played. Thousands upon thousands of chanting spectators jammed the roadside or hung from nearby trees and rooftops and 200 million more sat transfixed in front of their television screens in homes all across Europe. King Baudouin of Belgium, in the Royal Palace at Antwerp, ordered his aide to turn up the radio and French President Giscard d' Estaing blocked out the affairs of state to focus in on the more important drama unfolding on the road to Pra Loup.

Eddy Merckx, Belgian champion of champions, the invincible King of the Road on a bicycle was being crushed by a French farm boy and everyone wanted to see it. "Merckx will win his sixth Tour de France," the world press had confidently predicted 14 days and nearly 1600 miles earlier at the Tour start in Charleroi. Who else? Merckx was World champion, acknowledged even by his staunchest rivals as the best cyclist the world has ever known.

But now, in the last 7.5 kilometers of the day's 215 kilometer stage to Pra Loup, Merckx was smashed. He had been on the attack for nearly eight hours, unmercifully putting the pressure on his rivals in hopes that they would crack. Forcing the pace over five mountain passes, plunging and shuddering down the other sides at speeds not even a downhill skier could match, Merckx was a man driven by his will to win, his determination to prove that he would remain the best no matter what the odds.

He almost did. He gambled on his reputed invincibility and, perhaps now for the first time in his career, he lost. Head hanging and eyes glazed with fatigue, Merckx was losing—meter by agonizing meter—the tenuous one-minute lead he had worked so hard all day to build up. He had tried too hard. His mind had forced his legs beyond the limit and now the champion of the world was about to pay his dues.

The eyes of Europe were on the Frenchman who was steaming up from behind, the underdog who knew the champion was faltering and with newfound courage moved in for the kill. He caught Merckx with five kilometers to go, flew by him with scarcely a glance, and danced up the finish through the throngs of hysterical fans who rhythmically chanted his name: "The-ve-net, The-ve-net, The-ve-net!"

Bernard Thevenet, the simple, determined farmer's son from Burgundy, became a hero that day. His relentless, 15-day pursuit of Eddy Merckx over the cobblestones of Northern France, across the snowy Pyrenees and now into the rugged Alps finally paid off— he had brought the yellow jersey of race leadership back to France and his countrymen loved him for it.

For five years the best cyclists France and all of the rest of the world could produce had raced, humiliated, in the shadow of the great Belgian. He always won so decisively, rode so flawlessly, that the others could barely be considered more than just supporting actors. French pride had been hurt for too long and the easiest way to soothe the sting was to pretend that the Tour, after 62 years, no longer meant anything, that it had degenerated into an annoying extravagance that France was obliged to tolerate in the name of tradition.

But on the road to Pra Loup on that warm July day in 1975, all those rationalizations were forgotten. In just a few short kilometers all the passion the French have for bike racing was rekindled and a major chapter in the chronicle of one of the most legendary sporting events in history was written. An underdog, a Frenchman, was now leading the Tour de France.

And that's the way it stayed for the final seven days, 850 miles to the finish in Paris. More Europeans than ever before lined the roads to get a fleeting glimpse of the Burgundian in the yellow jersey, the man who restored French honor to the longest, toughest, most awesome event in sport.

The final day's stage was a 100-mile closed circuit race on Paris's Champs-Elysées. Seven hundred thousand spectators crushed into the area and, when it was over, Bernard Thevenet was awarded the final yellow jersey by one of his most appreciative fans, President Giscard d'Estaing.

And so ended the sixty-second Tour de France. For weeks before it started, for every day during its progress, and for months after it was over, stories of that tour permeated the European sporting press, television and radio. It was like a 21-game World Series or three weeks of Super Bowl madness played for six hours at a time every day.

Bicycle racing is to Europe what football is to America and, similarly, the spectators are fanatical. They not only follow the Tour de France but they watch bike races all over the world, thriving on the exploits and scandals of their heroes. They see the best compete nearly 300 times a year, racing 100 miles or more a day during the hot summer months and sprinting around and around steeply banked indoor velodromes for six days at a time during the long winter season. Like their American counterparts, they are as thrilled by an upset victory as they are bored by complete dominance of any one individual or team. It is the struggle and the spectacle that draws the crowds and there is probably more of that in bicycle racing than most football or baseball fans ever dreamed.

So far, Americans have not been saturated with or even exposed to the struggle and spectacle of modern competitive cycling. There is no telling whether we could ever really be moved by an event like the Tour de France, a multi-day extravaganza that

Presse Sports

Seven Tours de France have been won by the first three men in the photo. Spanish rider, Luis Ocaña, shows the pain of the pace, while Merckx and Thevenet follow closely during the 1975 Tour de France.

Robert F. George

Oliver Martin wins the Cookshire Criterium stage of the Tour of the East Stage Race, Quebec, Canada, 1973. The race, consisting of seven stages, or 400 miles, was won by the American team.

spectators can only see for a few brief moments from the side of the road.

But Americans have loved bike racing before, the kind that can be watched in all its intricacies from one place—a seat at the velodrome. Six-Day races in Madison Square Garden and half-mile handicaps at the Newark Velodrome often drew larger crowds than Babe Ruth did at Yankee Stadium. In the twenties and thirties, American racers were the fastest and richest in the world, disdaining trips to Europe in favor of $1000-a-day contracts to ride the Sixes in cities from Topeka to Boston. Those days faded away as Depression, war, and the new love of the automobile combined to end America's passionate affair with the wheelmen.

But now cycling is coming back. Americans are once again in love with the bicycle. New velodromes are springing up all across the country and more colorful athletes, informative commentators, topflight promotions, and instant replay are joining forces to bring it back into the mainstream of American sport. As that happens, spectators will want to know more about the people, the strategies, and the events that make cycling one of the most universally appealing spectator sports in the world.

The Life of the Athlete

The nice thing about becoming a cyclist is that a person doesn't have to be a candidate for a sideshow in order to reach the top. The giants find their way to basketball, and the blockhouses shine on the gridiron, but the best cyclists in the world come from among the vast numbers of people of average height and build.

The top riders can always be picked out at a race before it even starts. Even the uninitiated observer cannot help but notice the professional air and well-prepared look of the real champions. Tanned and lean with sinewy bodies and smoothly shaved legs, well-trained cyclists pedal with fluid grace—crisply when they are warming up and like powerful piston engines during effort. The road riders—endurance specialists—have remarkably underdeveloped shoulders and arms in relation to the size of their barrel-like thighs and the amount of muscle definition flashes at each turn of the pedals. They must have no excess weight, no upper body bulk to slow them down over the mountains.

Racing at the Trexlertown velodrome is a spectacular event for thousands.

Most track sprinters, on the other hand, are built for explosive effort and possess enough upper body strength to easily destroy all but the strongest steel handlebars. Steve Woznick, triple National champion and Pan-Am Gold medalist is a case in point. He is powerfully built and disdains the lightweight aluminum bars preferred by road racers: "I turn them into pretzels," he says.

Of course those are the two extremes—the thin, emaciated climbing specialist, and the stocky, volatile master of short explosive efforts on the velodrome. Most good cyclists fall somewhere in between and all learn quickly how best to use their talents in all types of events.

Roger Young, perhaps the best current all-round cyclist in the United States, exemplifies the new breed of serious, determined American racers. As a 22-year-old National Team member and candidate for his second Olympic team, Young is on his way up in international cycling. "I want to be respected as one of the best in the world," he says, "I want to see just how far I can go." To do that, Young, like other dedicated athletes, must sacrifice a lot. He is taking about seven years to complete his

studies in veterinary medicine and spends so much time traveling
that he rarely has a chance to unpack his suitcase.

He is primarily a track specialist—a very fast and snappy
pedaler with quick acceleration and a lot of endurance. At first
glance he doesn't look at all like he would possess the power of
some of the more muscular, bulky track riders—sprinters who
bend handlebars and seem always to be supercharged with energy.

Roger Young and his father Clair at the Northbrook, Illinois velodrome.

Robert F. George

Roger Young and Jesus Portalatin in a Match Sprint during the 1973 National Track Championships in Northbrook, Illinois, 1973.

Robert F. George

Roger Young beating Jack Disney in the Sprint during Nationals' competition at Northbrook, Illinois, 1973.

He is slightly built and round-shouldered, enough so to make him seem somewhat shorter than his actual height of five-feet ten-inches. He only weighs 140 pounds and it's easy to understand why his teammates affectionately call him "the Gnat." But there is an amazing contrast in Young's physical appearance. The slender, finely featured, low-keyed image he projects when fully clothed, disappears the moment he dons his racing uniform. Suddenly he becomes all legs. His short, slender torso is incongruously mounted on a pair of long, thick, incredibly muscular pistons that understandably give him the power to sprint faster than most of his competitors.

Young's talent is, in fact, his leg speed. He uses it to win championship match sprints. He was National Sprint champion in 1973. He was a key member of the U.S. Gold medal winning quartet at the 1975 Pan-American Games. In addition, he thrills the crowd with his leg speed on the indoor board tracks of Europe every winter.

He loves the excitement of track racing but he also has shown considerable talent in short distance road races. "Young is the complete bike rider," says Olympic track coach Jack Simes, "He can go hard for a long time and still outsprint almost everyone at the end. He'd make a good pro."

Young, like most of the top American riders, might want to become a professional someday. Right now that's pretty unlikely for at least a while because in order to do so, an American must try to break into the tough European circuit on his own. It's like expecting a missionary to fit right in with a tribe of hungry cannibals. Young is doing the next closest thing, however. He spends several months each winter riding amateur Six-Day races in Belgium and, because of his light flashy style, he has become quite popular with the European fans.

So Young's program is to spend the winter in Belgium racing his bicycle. Very few top American cyclists are able, or even want, to make that much of a sacrifice. Most work during the winter at odd jobs to save enough money to get themselves started on the long March-to-November U.S. season. Although officially classified as amateurs, if they ride well, like Young, they will collect enough in expense money, prizes, and sponsor support to keep going throughout the year. If they crash too frequently, get sick, or just don't finish in the top few places each race, they must confine their travels to their own areas and suffer the consequences of losing out on the best competition.

Right now Roger Young is on top. He is good enough to win or place in just about every race he enters and, consequently, the prizes he gets and the expense money promoters and sponsors give him more than pay for his travel to all the best races in the country. After two weeks of rest in Detroit from the winter season in Belgium, he heads down to Florida with 30 or 40 clubmates to begin road training in the warm sun. "We stay there for a couple of weeks," he says. "I try to put on 60 to 100 miles a day, just pedaling without a lot of hard pushing."

A lot of the eastern and midwestern riders do the same thing to escape the lingering northern snows and a whole series of early season races has developed to accommodate them. Most of these are road races, long two-day affairs like the 235-mile Cross Florida Tour or the demanding Olympic Development Tour of Tallahassee. Although he often places in the top five in these events, Young rides them only for training. The winners are usually members of the National Road team who are preparing for major international stage races like the 12-day Tour of Baja in Mexico or the equally long Tour of Britain later in the season.

By the time he leaves Florida in early April, Young will have ridden a total of 2,500 miles in three months. That's a good solid endurance base from which he can begin to concentrate on developing the speed he will have to have for the track racing that starts in June.

The Criterium

April and May are peppered with weekend criteriums, the most lucrative and popular road events on the calendar. When Young shows up for one of these, like the "Tour of Somerville," a 50-mile New Jersey classic, he is always considered a pre-race favorite. His reputation precedes him—virtually all of the 15,000 licensed U.S. racers know what he has done from having seen him ride or from having read about his many exploits in the two na-

Roger Young winning the Tour of Somerville in 1972. Sheila Young, his sister, is in the background, jumping in her excitement.

tional racing publications they avidly devour every month. "When Roger is on," one of his competitors once said, "nobody can touch him."

That's certainly true. In 1972, Young won the Tour of Somerville against the best in the country. He did it the way he knows best—by winning the final sprint against 14 other riders in the lead group. In addition to Somerville, he has won criteriums in cities like Los Angeles, Chicago, Detroit, Miami, and Philadelphia at distances ranging from 35 to 100 miles.

Criteriums are exciting events for spectators to watch and some of the older classics, like Somerville, draw crowds of nearly 30,000. They are generally held on city streets or in parks where the one-half to two-mile circuits can be blocked off from traffic. They are colorful and fast, with enough twisting turns and determined contestants to challenge even the best bike handlers and tacticians.

Roger Young likes criteriums. There is plenty of excitement, a lot of atmosphere, and a chance to win better prizes than in any other type of event. And there's the crowd. At a good criterium the

Robert F. George

Thousands of spectators attend Criteriums, such as the Somerville race pictured here, to watch hundreds of racers of all ages from all sections of the country.

spectators really get involved; they line the circuit and, urged on by the announcer, offer special "prime" prizes for extra sprints during the race. "Lots of times I don't feel up to riding a particular event," Young says, "but when I get in there, and I hear the crowd, and I hear the primes, something clicks inside. I really want to go for it."

He is drawn as if by a magnet to Belgium each year. He gets a thrill out of competing before a stomping, cheering crowd at the Ghent Sportspalais every night—the kind of cycling atmosphere that Americans haven't seen since the days of the Sixes in Madison Square Garden.

Young is a performer. He thrives on the cheers of the fans and there's nothing he likes better than being regarded as a classy rider with a flair for winning close finishes. Off the bike you'd never know it—he's quiet, withdrawn, and very intense about his preparation and his desire to perform well. He seldom discusses his inner feelings about the sport but, when he comes off the track after winning a close sprint and the roar of the crowd is still ringing in his ears, there is a fire in his eyes that says it all.

The Sprint

It's only natural that Roger Young is drawn to track events. His speed is best expressed there, his talents are recognized by the audience, and there is a velodrome not too far from where he grew up.

So when June rolls around, Young gets out his trackbike and starts to sharpen up on the kind of speed he will need for the National Sprint Championships. The road training and the criteriums he has ridden have made him very fit but they have also dulled the sting of his sprint. That sprint is a finely honed thing—it easily loses its edge from too many miles, too much slogging of big gears on the road. It must be brought back by short, snappy workouts on the track. When he starts to pedal like a sewing machine instead of a jackhammer, Young knows that his sprint is coming back.

In order to qualify for the National Championships, all licensed riders must compete in district qualification meets. The winners become district champions and receive expense money to help get to the Nationals. Young breezes through the Michigan qualifications every year, saving his real concentration and effort for the test he will face when the best riders in the nation come together to battle it out for titles in the seven senior events.

Of the track events, the sprint is the most prestigious, the most exciting, and the one Roger Young most likes to win. He was champion in 1973, second place in 1974 and third place in 1975. The winner those last two years was Steve Woznick, the burly, headstrong crusher from New Jersey who has the best finish of any of America's sprinters. Young has an excellent jump, and a good top end, but he can't quite match Woznick's final kick at the finish. They are both clever and quick. They have to be to make it to the finals.

"Sprinting is like a high-speed chess match; there's no room for mistakes," says Jack Simes, himself no stranger to the highly tactical battle of skill, speed, and nerves. In a 45-mile-per-hour sprint, a slight miscalculation or a subtle flick of an opponent's bike is often all it takes to lose an advantage or, in many cases, a lot of skin.

It's a lot different from sprint events in running or swimming where the contestants stay in lanes and go flat out from the gun. Of

Robert F. George

Steve Woznick battling Roger Young at the National Championships in Northbrook, Illinois.

Robert F. George

Steve Woznick and Hans Nuerenberg racing at the Kenosha velodrome in Wisconsin.

course sprints in cycling—two- or three-up matches—are held on steeply banked velodromes that allow competitors to maintain top speed without losing traction in the turns.

The first two laps of the three-lap event generally develop as a slow motion game of cat and mouse. It is usually suicidal to attempt outsprinting an adversary from the gun because the slower rider off the mark can simply tuck in behind, save his enery for nearly the entire distance and then, as the pacemaker tires, pull out and sprint by for an easy victory.

Perhaps it is appropriate here to clarify cycling's most prevalent tactic—the art of sitting-in. A rider moving at a speed above about 10-miles-per-hour creates a still pocket of air directly behind him which another rider can tuck or "sit" into to minimize effort. The lead rider is breaking the wind or "pulling pace" while the following rider is exerting about 15 percent less effort by "sitting-in."

So if a sprinter makes his move too early, his opponent, by tucking-in closely enough, can take advantage of that pocket or slipstream to save effort for as long as possible. The following rider, of course, is much fresher at the finish and much more likely to have the energy for that final burst to the line.

So the character and tactics of a cycling match sprint take on a whole new perspective. The first and second laps consist of feinting and faking maneuvers to get into position for that final drive to the finish. Only the last 200 meters of the sprint is timed.

Young usually prefers to ride his matches from the rear, slowing and stalling, sometimes even coming to a complete standstill in order to force his opponent to take the lead. He is clever and, from the rear position, can watch his adversary's every move—ready to take advantage of a look over the wrong shoulder or an awkward moment when pedals are in a straight up and down position.

Other sprinters, like Pan-Am Bronze medalist Carl Leusenkamp, prefer the front position, daring an opponent to get by. Of course there are rules against flagrant impediment of a rival's attempts to pass around the outside but Leusenkamp has the ability to make that distance quite a bit longer than normal. He keeps his opponent high on the banking for as long as he can on the final lap, stalling the sprint until the last possible moment. The shorter the better for Leusenkamp. His acceleration or "jump" is hard to

Jack Simes engaged in a battle of wits with Australian champion Gordon Johnson.

An expert racer is able to bring his bike to a complete stop, balancing on the track and forcing his opponent into the lead.

Robert F. George

Carl Leusenkamp, on the inside of the sprinter's lane, forces John Chapman higher on the slope of the track.

match and many sprinters who need a longer distance to get to top speed have fallen prey to this successful tactic.

The subtleties of the sprint tactics of men like Young, Woznick, and Leusenkamp are what make sprinting on a bicycle so unique and exciting. The year Woznick took away Young's title, the two final rides were photofinishes, Woznick winning the championship by less than a centimeter. The roar of the crowd was louder than ever and, even though Young had lost, he knew he had put up a good fight.

The next year, 1975, he put up a good fight too, but this time he was beaten by two men and had to settle for the Bronze. The competition was getting fiercer each year and Young, in order to get the chance to compete in the Pan-American Games, had to make a compromise. After the Nationals he switched to the team pursuit, a 4000-meter four-man event that is the ultimate in cycling speed and precision. At first he didn't like the idea of having to depend on three other people—he preferred the satisfaction of winning on his own. "I felt like a second-class citizen in the team pursuit," he said, "but I wanted to make a strong contribution."

The Team Pursuit

The team pursuit is an event that grows on a cyclist. It is fast, exciting, technical, and, if it's done right, incredibly exhilarating. The distance is 4,000 meters, two and one-half miles of maximum effort around the velodrome. The object of the event is to go as fast as possible and try to catch or gain an advantage over an opposing team starting on the other side of the track. The riders on each team are held four abreast for the start and drop into single file immediately after the race begins. Tucked one behind the other in perfect formation, the job of pacing is rotated every half or full lap, the front man ending his "pull" by swinging straight up the banking and dropping back down inches behind the last man. The riders must spend hours of training time together in order to perfect those precision change-offs and get to know each other's distinctive riding styles. They must be as equal in speed and smoothness as possible, for even the slightest fluctuation in pace or unexpected waver can throw off a team's rhythm and destroy a good ride.

The 1975 Pan-Am Pursuit team was perfection on wheels. Young fit in nicely. His smooth and fast pedaling style plus his spectacular sense of timing in the change-offs made him a solid member of the quartet. They trained together for four weeks under the strict and knowing eye of team coach Jack Simes. "By the night of the finals they were ready to roll," he said. "They looked like West Germans."

Robert F. George

United States Pan-American Pursuit team which won a Gold medal in Mexico City in 1975. Paul Deem leads, followed by Roger Young, Paul Therrio, and Ron Sharin.

They did, in fact, look as well-drilled and smooth as any pursuit team in the world. Simes was at trackside closely monitoring their pace against the powerful Colombians, the team they had to beat for the Gold medal. Using prearranged signals and a clever strategy, he held them back for nine laps to let the South American favorites think they had a winning advantage. With three laps remaining, Simes gave the signal to open it up, and the quartet responded by closing the gap and rocketing on to a one and one-half second advantage at the finish. Never did they falter or lose their rhythm. Four men were riding as one at speeds over 35 miles an hour with barely inches separating their wheels—each going flat out with no fear of the slightest waver. "That was the ultimate," said California team member Paul Deem, "I wanted to go on like that all night."

It's that kind of moment that a cyclist lives for. All the sacrifices, all the training, the living out of suitcases, the months and years of preparation all seem worthwhile for that fleeting instant when it all comes together.

Popular Track Events

The *Miss and Out* is a regular feature at velodromes throughout the world. In England it is appropriately called "Devil Take the Hindmost" because at the conclusion of each lap, the last rider to cross the line is called out. Riders are removed until there are three left to contest the final sprint. A good "devil" will tell the spectator a lot about the personalities of the racers. The endurance rider protects himself by setting a fast, even pace at the front while the crafty, explosive sprinters will delight in eliminating riders by slipping by them at the last possible moment. It is an enjoyable race for the riders, but one that requires stamina, judgment, and good bike handling.

Another popular event at most velodromes, especially in Europe, is the *Handicap*. The three-lap race is extremely fast with riders starting only several meters apart, according to their past performance record. The last and fastest rider gets the title of "scratchman," while the slowest rider is known as the "limit man." If the handicap has been computed properly, all riders will reach the finish at the same time. The one with the best kick will win.

Robert F. George

Miss and Out race at the East Point, Georgia velodrome.

Miss and Out race at Trexlertown as seen from the infield.

Robert F. George

Cyclists warming up behind a derney at a Montreal velodrome.

Spectator view of the start of a Handicap race, where riders are "spread out" around the oval track according to their ability and to previously posted times.

"Bird's-eye" view of the start of a Handicap race, taken with a fish-eye lense from one of the velodrome light platforms. As is customary at bicycle tracks, the riders "camp" in the infield, waiting for their events.

Start of a mass start Scratch race at the Trexlertown, Pennsylvania velodrome.

Robert F. George

A rider taking a spill at the Northbrook velodrome.

Also standard fare at most velodromes is the popular *Points* race. The winner of this race is not necessarily the rider who crosses the line first on the final lap. Instead, it is the rider who has scored the most points during special sprints throughout the race. In a five-mile points race, for example, riders would collect points for placing in the sprints every mile. At the end of the race points are added and the winner named.

Motor-Paced Racing, once very popular in America, is still featured at velodromes across the world. The driver and his motorcycle are called "gangmakers," while the rider tucked in behind is called the "stayer." Small motors, called "dernies," buzz around the velodromes at speeds up to 40 miles an hour. The big motors are more specialized, belt-driven machines. The drivers straddle their machines in a standing position assuring maximum wind protection for the "stayer." Speeds up to 70 miles an hour can be reached by a racer behind the big motors.

Less raucous, but nevertheless quite exciting, are the numerous variations of the individual and team Pursuits. The *Italian Pursuit* is like a team Pursuit except that a team can include any number of riders from two to ten. Instead of the team finishing together, each rider does his one lap turn at the front and then pedals off, leaving the last man of each team to battle it out for the victory. The *Australian Pursuit* is a demanding race. The winner is the rider who has the endurance and speed to catch his opponent, or sometimes three or four opponents, starting at points equidistant from one another around the track.

Putting several of these events together with a point system determining the overall placings of selected participants, creates what is called an *Omnium*. Usually, six or ten invited riders score points in a mixture of events such as a *Miss and Out*, a *Kilometer Time Trial*, a *Points Race*, and a *Pursuit*. Events will depend on the type of riders competing.

The Uniqueness of Cycling

Bicycle racing is an oddity. For an American, cycling is sometimes hard to understand because it just doesn't fit into the mold of our favorite sporting pastimes. It is not a game that is played between two structured teams that hustle back and forth between goals. It is a race, but not the straightforward contest observed between swimmers, runners, or horses. It depends upon sophisticated equipment and machines, but there are no motors or sails. It is a skill sport, but one that requires incredible physical training as well as hours of practice.

The participants, the athletes, are recognizable. They have the determination, the drive, and the intensity that characterizes all competitors in individual sports. But there is something more, something extra, that draws and holds people to cycling. Few cyclists can ever really quit. They make comebacks, they become officials or coaches, or they just ride right into their seventies and eighties. They may get involved in every other type of sport and activity but they always seem to come back.

There is a reason for it somewhere. Maybe it's the great number and variation of cycling events; it's normal for races to be held at distances from one-quarter mile to over 2,000 miles. Or it could be the lure of cycling's intricate strategies and tactics—the unique elements of the sport that make victory dependent on things like wind protection and technical efficiency as well as speed, stamina, and cleverness.

Maybe, too, it's the equipment. Ever since it was first conceived, the bicycle has been a lure—an amazing device that allows man to travel under his own power with the greatest speed and efficiency. Anyway, a discussion of the machine is a good place to begin.

Over the years racing bikes have been redesigned, refitted, and, streamlined to the point where the finest now weigh less than 20 pounds and are still able to withstand skittering 60 mile-per-hour descents down treacherous mountain roads.

The top racers have at least several of these frail-looking machines. Eddy Merckx, professional cycling's ace of aces, keeps a ready stable of 15 and is so particular about their adjustment that he has been known to tinker with his saddle position while careening down the sides of mountains.

For road races the bikes are outfitted with gears, brakes, and waterbottles and, when the riders roll along the road their machines make a merry tinkling and clicking sound. Not so merry are the racers who have to have at least 10 speeds and sometimes 12 to

Road Bike. Note the brakes, gear sprocket, and water bottle.

The track bike has a fixed gear and no brakes.

get over agonizing mountain passes. The bikes have hard, narrow saddles, painstakingly selected to allow as much comfort as possible for up to eight hours of constant pedaling at a time.

A racer's feet are strapped into the pedals and held immobile by a deep-grooved cleat that is mounted on the bottom of special shoes with light, but stiff steel-reinforced soles. If the foot should slip out, seconds, and races, can be lost. If a rider crashes, he must learn to slide with his bike.

The racers appreciate their bicycles but, for them, they are more a means to an end than masterpieces of handcrafted mechanical genius that elicit "oohs" and "ahs" from admiring novices. The builders and the mechanics are the ones who put love into a fine bicycle. They are forever tinkering with them—trying to find better ways to lighten tubing, delicately file lugs, or fine-tune components. As a result, the cost of the custom-made bicycle goes up and up. The most expensive now approach $1,200 and tires alone cost $30 apiece. Frame tubes are specially cut according to a rider's size and weight. Angles, dimensions, and flexibility are changed according to the specific event for which the bike will be used.

As the 10- or 12-speed road racing machine approaches the ultimate in self-propelled mechanical genius, so the stripped down, super-efficient track bike epitomizes mechanical simplicity. It is nothing but frame, wheels, handlebars, saddle, and pedals. There are no brakes, no gear-changing mechanisms and no water bottles. The track bike is built strictly for speed. It is short, steep, and rigid—designed to flash its rider up and down velodrome bankings at 40 miles per hour. The wheels are extremely light and tires are made out of silk and inflated to 150 pounds per square inch. There is no freewheeling or braking—the rider slows down by resisting the pedals or applying a gloved hand to the front wheel. The sound such a bike makes as it hurtles around the track is magical. There is no motor, no roar, just the sound of expanding, straining lungs, air rushing by, and a rhythmic whooshing of hard tires on rumbling boards.

It's true that the gleaming, fragile-looking machines and the distinctive sounds they make create a tremendous amount of atmosphere at a bike race. They evoke the same kind of feelings a baseball fan experiences when he hears the thumping of a glove or the crack of a bat. But sounds and images are only part of an athletic show. The appreciation of a well-executed double play, the impact of a 60-yard end zone bomb, or the masterful setup of a game-winning slap shot are the things that give each sport its unique character and appeal.

On the stage to Pra Loup, for example, it was Thevenet's mastery of the situation that gave his win such impact. The ability he had to let the champion dangle without panicking and the fantastic timing he used to administer the death blow in the final two miles of a 135-mile race is what really turned Europe on. It was a beautiful display of athletic prowess in a sport that they understand.

Cycling tactics and strategies are complex and fascinating. They are hard to explain to a person who doesn't have a feel for the sport. As an American grows up knowing that a baseball game lasts nine innings, so a European understands that bicycle races often go on for 21 days. It's just part of life. Knowledge of the fine points of any game is gradually acquired and seldom is there a fan who actually sits down and memorizes the official rule book.

An interesting discussion of cycling tactics, then, cannot really go much beyond illustrating some of the basic principles involved. Recall that the unique aspects of a cycling match sprint, for example, revolve around the concept of "sitting-in" or using an opponent as a wind break so that effort can be saved for as long as possible. This one feature of bicycle racing—the fact that sitting-in is much easier than setting the pace—is the principle that underlies nearly all of cycling's complex tactics and strategies.

There is only one type of event that is exempt from the sitting-in pulling-pace phenomenon—the individual time trial. It is known as the test of truth, the measure of an athlete on a machine against his own willpower and the clock. Some riders love it; they say it is the only real measure of cycling prowess. Most racers hate it; it is unexciting, unimaginative, and extremely painful.

There is only one individual time trial that really matters in the cycling world anyway, and that's the world hour record.

Eddy Merckx, the man who has won the Tour de France five times, been World champion four times, and won more classics than any other bike rider ever, said after he broke that record in 1972: "This is my greatest achievement. I am more proud of this than any of my other victories." On the Olympic Velodrome in Mexico City, Merckx pedaled an astounding 49.43 kilometers in exactly one hour. King Baudouin and the whole Belgian royal family had flown in for the occasion and millions of Europeans watched Merckx pedal around that track alone for nearly 28 miles. Boring? Ridiculous? Maybe, but nevertheless the supreme tribute to his ability. No other cyclist in the world can do what Merckx did that day. "I will never try it again," he said. "It was too hard."

Of course watching most anybody else but Merckx attempting that kind of record seems ludicrous. Time trials, whether they be for a world record attempt or for a National 25-Mile Championship on the road are just not that interesting to watch.

It is when racers are pitted against one another that the sport becomes exciting. Factors like cleverness, cunning, agility, and timing come into play, and when racers are of similar abilities and at similar levels of fitness, the wizened veterans usually steal the show.

At the 1975 National Road Championships, for example, John Howard, former champion and seasoned international competitor, knew just what he had to do to win the 125-mile event. He sat-in for the first 100 miles and calmly watched the others chip away at their reserves by attacking and chasing each other in dozens of abortive moves. With 20 miles left, he launched the one big attack he had been saving all day and only two other riders had enough energy to respond. He eventually dropped them and finished alone over a minute ahead. He knew what he had to do and he played his cards right.

Howard was in his element that day. He is a road rider and the longer and harder the race, the better he will do. He has to ride differently when he gets into criteriums, though—the shorter "round the houses" races that favor sprinters like Young or Woznick. "Howie tries to burn me off," says Woznick, "because if I'm there at the finish he knows I'll zap him." Woznick likes to play with the road riders in those types of events. At the 50-mile Coconut Grove criterium in Florida one year he was in a seven-man breakaway that contained Howard and several of the nation's best endurance men. "They were so dumb," Woznick said, "I told them I was lapped and they were stupid enough to believe me." They towed him around for 30 miles and when he suddenly blasted through at the finish they realized they'd been had. "Anybody who doesn't know who's been lapped and who hasn't, deserves to lose," Woznick said.

So sitting-in, using the wheels, and sometimes pulling a fast one on your opponents are all part of the game. But riders like Woznick or Howard aren't champions only because they're cagey; they have a tremendous amount of fitness and determination to back it up. They are the first ones to admit that the best bike races are won by the strongest and most aggressive competitors. Said Woznick after a trip to Holland where the amateur races are considered the toughest in the world: "I thought I'd get into a few criteriums and, you know, sit-in for awhile and then win a few primes. Well, I never even *smelled* the front of the field, they went so hard. I finished one race out of ten and I didn't win a dime in six weeks."

That's the way it is in Europe. They still have the toughest and hardest races in the world. It's more of a team sport over there, too, with members of the same sponsored group or club or national team working together to keep as many victories as possible in the family. The big stage races and the international tours are where teamwork most obviously comes into play. In professional races, like the Tour de France, the aces are the team leaders, surrounded and taken care of on the road by *"domestiques"*—excellent racers themselves who are paid handsomely for the sacrifice. The better they are at helping their leader win races, the more they get paid. They are like the linesman in professional football, the unsung heroes who open the holes for the runners, protect the quarterback and do any of the dog work left over to make sure the stars get on the front page. In cycling, good *domestiques* give up their food, their bicycles, and even their own chances for victory on their leader's request. They pace him back to the field if he has had trouble, they neutralize attacks by rival team leaders and they shelter him from strong headwinds.

Of course in the United States teamwork is seldom, if ever, taken that far. But it does exist and, with more sponsors anxious to see their name on the jerseys of the winners, the more likelihood there is of combinations forming. It makes the racing interesting and adds another dimension to the game.

On the East Coast, the Paris Sport team had the best combine going for several years. Woznick (a sprinter), Chapman (a team pursuiter), and Cooney (a road rider) clicked well together. Of course, if the race came down to a sprint finish, Woznick, as National Sprint champion, would be the man, and the other two would lead him out for the final dash. On the last lap Cooney would hit the front to pick up the tempo, Chapman followed with Woznick glued to his wheel and then, with about 100 meters to go the Woznick would uncork his final, victorious blast to the tape. Sometimes Cooney or Chapman would get off the front early in the race and Woznick would do everything he could to abort opponents' efforts at organizing an effective chasing unit. "It was a lot of fun," said Woznick, "we won a lot of races and we split the prizes right down the middle. Pretty soon everybody else started trying it and then it *really* got to be fun."

Whether in an amateur criterium in America or in the big time Tour de France, tactics are a large part of the game. Sitting-in, lead-outs, breakaways—they all add an exciting dimension to a race. It's what makes sprints in cycling more than just a dash to the tape or road races merely a contest of who can go the fastest for the longest time. They add color, flavor, and excitement to the sport and they make the events much more interesting to watch.

And, speaking of events, there are more different types of those in cycling than in any other sport. Stage races, time trials, sprints, pursuits, motor-paced, Madisons—the list goes on and on. Some of them are official World championship and Olympic title events. If a rider wins one of those he or she gets a Gold medal and the exclusive right to wear the most coveted vest of all—the Rainbow Jersey of the World champion. It's beautiful—all white with the colors of the rainbow around the chest. Sprinter Daniel Morelon of France has won seven of them. Eddy Merckx, king of the professional road-racing elite, has won four. American men haven't won any for over 40 years.

Some of the traditional championship races have already been mentioned; the match sprint, the team pursuit, the road. In track

"Cornering" during a Team Time Trial in Concord, Massachusetts.

racing, there is also the kilometer time trial, the individual pursuit and, in America, the ten mile.

The kilometer is Woznick's favorite event. It is short, simple, pure, and incredibly painful: "You have to put everything, I mean *everything*, into that one minute of effort. It's just you, your bike, and your ability to power through that pain barrier."

It's just one man against the clock for six-tenths of a mile from a standing start. No sweat. But the best coaches in the world say it takes eight days to recover from a properly ridden kilometer. And there's really only one way to tell if you've done it right: "You do it the way Trentin did when he won the Olympic Gold medal in 1968," Woznick says. "When he finished, he passed out."

The individual pursuit is like the kilometer in that it is ridden without the help of any teammates or any opponent's rear wheel. But it's four times as long (4,000 meters) and a lot easier to settle into a rhythm. The object of the pursuit is to try to gain an advantage by the end of the race on an opponent who starts on the opposite side of the track. As multi-national champion John Vande Velde put it, "A good pursuiter has to have everything: speed, endurance, a well-developed sense of pace, and the ability to focus concentration on nothing but going fast."

Good pursuiters and good kilometer men are suited to other events as well. Take the ten mile, for example. It is a National championship event on the track and is always the grand finale of the yearly program. All the senior riders jump into it—sprinters, kilometer men, pursuiters, and it's usually a blistering affair. The winner often takes it by mere inches.

There are literally dozens of other track and road events held on velodromes and on road courses throughout the world. The best of these are products of each individual promoter's own ingenuity with "home rules" always included to add a little extra spice.

The one event, above all others, that captured all the elements of competitive cycling was the Six-Day. During their peak years in the twenties and thirties, Six-Day races often had fans going wild until two in the morning.

In the United States today, the Six-Day has been virtually replaced by the ever popular, usually one-hour or 25-mile event known as the Team Race or Madison. Team races are held as a

Robert F. George

Steve Woznick starting a championship Kilometer ride at the Kenosha, Wisconsin track.

regular feature at most velodromes across the country, with up to
30 riders in two- or three-man teams on the track at one time. "A
good team race has everything the crowd wants," says Jack Simes,
"color, excitement, speed, bike handling. It's all there."

They can certainly be hairy at times, too. Both teammates are
on the track for the entire race, although only one at a time is
actually racing. This man, after riding flat out for between one and
three laps, will relay his partner into the race by a powerful hand-
sling or specially executed shove to the left hip. He then slowly
circles around the top of the track, resting until he is again "picked
up" by his partner.

Because each partner has frequent chances to rest, the overall
speed of the race is sizzling and those high speed relay changes or
"pickups" make for a spectacular show of bike handling and beauti-
fully timed effort.

A team wins if it succeeds in lapping all the other teams on the
track or if it has accumulated the highest number of points for placing in numerous sprints during the race. "In a good team race
you're going all the time," Roger Young says. "You've got to be
quick and strong and, man, when you go for that lap you've got to
put everything into it. It's either flat-out or pack up and go home.
There's no backing out."

CHAPTER FOUR

Women on the Wheel

ALICE KOVLER, JAMES C. MC CULLAGH

THE two women sat nervously on their bikes held in the iron grip of handlers. Sue Novara and Sheila Young straddled their machines in preparation for the match sprint at the Track Championships in Northbrook, Illinois. Although both had raced each other many times before, they appeared to be new rivals on the stage of the oval track. At the gun the women ambled forward, as they would for 800 meters, each trying to force the other into a dangerous lead. Skittishly, they moved high on the banking, rocking back and forth in their pedals and balancing their bikes like performers on the wire. Within a bike length of each other, they circled above the safety line keeping the track below them to allow a generous descent into speed. With the grace of a dancer, Novara stopped her bike for seconds, turning her pedals just enough to balance, and sending Young into the front. When the bell lap sounded Young swooped down to the bottom of the track and began her sprint to the tape. Novara followed like a cat. Sitting-in for 50 meters, Novara swept by Young to win by lengths. Thousands of spectators applauded two of America's finest women sprinters.

These women occupy central positions in an American sports paradox. How is it that women, deprived of adequate training facilities, often ignored by the cycling federation, and, at least in modern times, so new to international racing, have been able to score such noticeable success in world-class bicycle racing events?

Robert F. George

Sheila Young leads Sue Novara at Northbrook, Illinois.

If their success is the paradox, the irony is that they have received so little national attention. Heralded in Europe as the force to return women's cycling to its former prominence and to offset the Russians' mastery of the sport since 1958, the women are in large measure unheralded at home in spite of remarkable accomplishments.

Perhaps the most unexpected feature of the American cycling renaissance in the 1970s has been the emergence of a group of women riders who have earned six World championship medals, including three first-place Golds. During the same period only one man, Jack Simes, has taken a medal; a Silver in the Kilometer in 1968. It is a startling accomplishment, achieved with little help and encouragement from the male-dominated cycling authorities in the country.

In 1976 there are approximately 8,000 men in the United States Cycling Federation as compared to 500 women. While there are literally dozens of male riders capable of defeating any of the others on a given day, the serious women riders are few. At the top of any list are World champions Audrey McElmury (1969, Road Race), Sheila Young (1973, Sprint), and Sue Novara (1975, Sprint). After these would come Miji Reoch with her Silver medal in the Pursuit Race and other strong capable riders, including Jane Buyny, Jane Robinson, Sue Gurney, Linda Stein, and Barbara Amburgey. These are the riders who dominate competition, the elite of the road and the track.

The travails of a woman racer in the 1950s and 1960s have been detailed by Nancy Nieman in her book, *The Turned Down Bar*, an interesting account of, among other things, her experiences in European racing. Nieman, who was a track rider and one-time co-holder of the World 200-Meter record, ties the recent development of American racing to the construction of new tracks in the 1960s. When she raced there were exactly two in the country, compared to 12 in 1976, and well over 100 at the turn of the century. Racing for women was even less attractive than it is now, and simply getting to use the facilities was an achievement. There were no match sprints: the women simply raced in a "pack" whenever and wherever they could.

Nieman sees Audrey McElmury's 1969 World Road Championship win as the watershed for women's racing. Before this time, a woman could not extract travel expense money beyond a token amount. Sheila Young, who is a champion bike racer and speed skater (she was the first American to win three medals in the Winter Olympics, doing so in 1976), recalled the frustration of competing in international cycle events. When competing in the

World Cycling Championships in Marseilles, France, "I had to pay my own fare over and back." Her father has acknowledged that the keeping of his son and daughter in bike racing "keeps me broke."

The argument against funding women was based essentially on the fact that there were so few of them competing, and the dues paid by these amounted to very little. Against this argument, Nieman posed a sharper one: *Who is bringing home the medals?*

Eventually, McElmury's and Sheila Young's international victories loosened the purse strings, so that riders like Novara and Reoch would not have the same kind of difficulty being funded.

Nonetheless, the question remains. How have the American women been able to earn what the men are still waiting for: international success? If the key to winning bike races is suffering, as many top racers seem to agree, the American women have a great advantage over their male contemporaries. That advantage, paradoxically, comes from the general neglect of women in the sport and the absurdly short distances of many women's races, which are curtailed in length for the convenience of promoters and officials, and to some extent by tradition. Having no alternative, the women have frequently raced with the men, and they have learned to suffer.

A woman in a man's race, even a very ordinary contest, is in about the same position as an American male rider in a European race. She has virtually no chance to win: she is outclassed. Therefore, she must be extremely conscious of tactics just to stay in the field. Being physically outclassed, there is no margin for mental error. She must learn to accept the frustration of making a serious effort and going unrewarded. Many try and give up quickly, but those who stay in a men's race leave the experience with a priceless advantage. They learn how to function at the outer perimeter of their capability, and how to handle the physical and mental stresses this situation creates.

For many complex reasons women have risen to the challenge of world-class competition. Now it is time for everyone to step back and consider what a remarkable achievement this is. After all is said and done, European women have had the advantages of experience, exposure to more sophisticated coaching, organized teams, and a general public respect for bike racing. The Russian

Robert F. George

Sheila and Roger Young, National   **Sue Novara waiting for the start of a match**
Sprint Champions in 1973.   **sprint race at the Trexlertown track.**

women, like the Russian men, have great advantages in terms of government support. But Audrey McElmury, Sheila Young, Sue Novara, and Miji Reoch, though they have worked in a sport with scant public notice, have earned six World medals in seven years.

Sprinting with Sue Novara

Sue Novara is a willowy girl of 20 who does not look or sound like anyone's idea of a champion. Yet, she defeated all competitors in the 1975 World Sprint Championships. One of them was Sheila Young, winner in 1973, and a fellow member of the Wolverine-Schwinn Club of Detroit, which has produced many national champions.

Novara is neither amazed nor overwhelmed by her success, nor does it bulk very large in her thinking. At times she gives the impression that it somehow all happened by itself; training is not a grind for her. She seems to have moved naturally to the top of her demanding sport. "I like going fast," she said. "I like being fit. Cycling's fun even if you don't compete and just go out for rides in the country. It is something everyone should do. If I'm not racing, I go for a ride with people. I just like cycling."

There is something characteristically American about Novara's involvement in cycling. Although she has beaten the best female sprinters in the world who have cared to meet her on the banking, she sees her own racing in terms of health, personal commitment, and growth. She is a natural subject for American and European magazine articles, but admits she "is not in the sport for attention.

Robert F. George

Sue Novara donning National Championship jersey.

I'm in it for satisfaction; I like to ride bikes and I have always been the type of person who likes to give 100 percent. And the satisfaction comes when your family is happy. I get great satisfaction when someone comes up to my dad and congratulates him for the job I've done. He has put in a lot of work and doesn't get much recognition."

Unlike many world champions who surround their sport in a mystique and consider it an end in itself, Novara considers the sport as a means toward personal development. Racing has given her confidence in other areas of her life. She recalls when she "was in high school and I won the national championship. My English teacher always used to tell me that it was going to make me a better person, because I had to put in so much time to do one thing and really accomplish it."

Novara's participation in bicycle racing underlines the value and the beauty of a sport which is not yet troubled by big gates and intense media coverage. She is an energetic symbol of a natural woman who discovered early that a bike was an exciting machine. Riding led to racing but the central preoccupation didn't change: cycling was fun. And she has kept this attitude all the way to becoming World champion. For her, racing is not a business.

Although she rarely speaks of the sacrifices she must make for her racing career, she is a determined and eager athlete. Since Flint, Michigan, her hometown, does not have any track facilities, she is forced to improvise. She seems not at all disconcerted that Russian and European champions usually have a number of velodromes within a convenient distance. Like teammate Sheila Young, Novara has reached staggering heights by virtue of her willingness to suffer upon the open road.

Fantastic as it sounds, Novara admits that she does not "get on the track until June," well into the racing season. Prior to this, she trains with her father who paces her with his motorcycle. Their relationship is an example for grass-roots racing in this country.

"All of May," she explained, "we do speed-work. We'll ride 25 miles and within this distance we'll do six sprints of about a quarter-mile. And we'll get it up as fast as we can go, ending with a quick accleration and an extra kick. Starting in June, besides the sprinting on the road, I go every night to a driver training course which is almost like an oval course blocked off to traffic. Here I practice "jumping," quick acceleration from almost nothing to 25 miles an hour. Getting quick is really important. When my father blows his whistle, I jump."

Novara attributes much of her success to her father's pertinacity. She acknowledged that without him, she would never have trained so hard. "He went out on days that I didn't feel like going out at all. He'd get me out and make me practice. And it really paid off. When I lost the National Championships in 1973 he watched where I made my mistakes. He nagged me all winter about why I lost. He's got a lot of influence over what I do. He puts in as much time as I do. He's been almost everything."

Novara, utilizing makeshift training facilities which would amaze most foreign rivals, has earned the reputation as a fierce and knowledgeable competitor in the quintessence of track events, the match sprint. To her the sprint "is scary because sprinting is not just pure speed all the time. I found that out in the World's in Montreal, losing by one-tenth of a second. No matter how fast you are, if your opponent knows tactics, she can use them to her advantage. She can hold you back, go early, or tire you out. In a sprint you have 400 meters of thinking and tactics, then 200 meters of raw speed.

"The first part is just a battle of nerves. You try to think of what the other person is going to do. You plan you own moves, which you hope will work. And if one move doesn't work, if your opponent doesn't take the bait when you move your bike a certain way, you have to try another move. The last half is where the speed comes in. You give the race everything you've got and hope nobody passes you. You've got to be unpredictable."

And unpredictable Novara is. Dissatisfied with the slow pace of the World Championship Road Race in Belgium, Novara left the peloton kilometers from the finish. Buffeted by a strong wind and slowed by a final climb, she went for a win rather than for a more or less guaranteed second or third in the final sprint. But, unfortunately, she had attacked too early and was passed by other racers. She still managed to finish sixth.

Novara is a natural competitor, which she attributes to growing up with boys. She thinks women are fortunate to have men to train and race with. "Men are naturally stronger than women. In order to stay with them, we have to train hard and that makes us a little better than the women who train by themselves. Training with Jack Disney, eight-time National Sprint champion, has helped me a lot. I know that if I can stay with him, I can beat any girl in the world."

She has said very forcefully that "I want to beat the men. I don't want people to say, 'She was a good woman sprinter.' I want them to say 'good, period.' No one ever had to push me in this. I always loved it. I like racing. I like the people. And I like to win. That's the most fun. I want to win the World's a couple more times. I want to win it more than the Russians have. They've dominated it too long."

In spite of her great confidence and aggressiveness, Novara feels that "you don't need that much talent to be a bike rider. You just need a lot of hard work. And a lot of determination." Through talent, work, and determination, Novara has become the fastest woman sprinter in the world. Although she admits to taking up sprinting for herself, she acknowledges that she "feels pride when they play our national anthem when you are up on the victory stand."

On the Road with Miji Reoch

Mere months after regular riding, Miji Reoch won the National championship on the road. She had little background in athletics other than tennis and surfing. She shocked the field and the American racing community. But she remains modest about her feat. "It was probably," she remarked, "the last year that someone new could do something like that. How, I don't know. Women's races in this country traditionally have not been that aggressive. I didn't think the race was really that hard a ride. It was only the third race I was in."

The story of how Miji Reoch became interested in bicycle racing at the age of 24 could provide solace to men and women of similar or older ages who question their ability to enter regular competition.

Vacationing in Milan, Italy with her husband, she purchased at his instigation a 10-speed custom bike. She knew nothing about

Robert F. George

Sue Novara and Sheila Young in the final 200 meters of their sprint.

Sue Novara "in traffic" during an Omnium event at Trexlertown.

Robert F. George

Robert F. George

Sue Novara leading Sue Gurney in a Match Sprint.

Sue Novara "on the wheel" of Russia's Tamara Pilschikova.

Robert F. George

Robert F. George

Reoch racing in Time Trial Championships in 1975 in Knellsville, Wisconsin.

Robert F. George

oung leads Tsareva of Soviet Union uring World Cycling Championships Montreal, Canada.

Reoch racing with men during Olympic Development Stage Race.

gears, speeds, or sprockets. Desiring people to ride with, she joined the Pennsylvania Bicycle Club. "I did well," she recalled, "on their training ride, and they really ride hard. The men in the club asked me if I wanted to race. Well, I really didn't know anything about racing but they started sending in entry blanks for me. Since we didn't have a car, they would take me to races.

"When I found out how much fun it was to win, I started spending more time, and more money on cycling. And my involvement escalated. In another way, it was easier for me. Because I started late, I never had to give up dating or had to choose between college and cycling. I am putting off children for racing."

Though she is quite happy to ride with the men and, indeed, attributes much of her strength to her training with the male pack, she has come to recognize the limitations in women's racing. "Recognition," she acknowledges, "is minimal. In addition, there are a lot of problems with women getting prizes. Sometimes the better women will ride with the men, and come out not getting any prizes because they will have been awarded in the token women's event of five or ten miles. That will be where all the prizes are awarded. On the other hand, most of the serious women riders want to ride the men's races. So you have to choose between the prizes and the training value, which can cause problems."

Rapidly earning a reputation as a hard, highly competitive rider in the individual pursuit and road events, Reoch perceives racing as a sport which pushes her to her limits. Reoch believes that "women traditionally haven't been aggressive and don't know how much their bodies can stand. I think women can withstand more pain than men. I know my husband brought out a lot of competition in me. On our rides he always pushes me and makes me fight for my own position. When I started riding I didn't care if I was the first one over the hill. And when I rode with women, they seemed to ride at an acceptable pace. But the men; they are always sprinting for the city limits sign."

Reoch understands pain and what her body can tolerate. To get herself in shape she does circuit training, which is a series of calisthenics involving different muscle groups but always taxing the heart. She likes "to train twice a day, at least twice a week. One session might be close to two hours, and the other session might be two and a half. I don't believe in not riding at all."

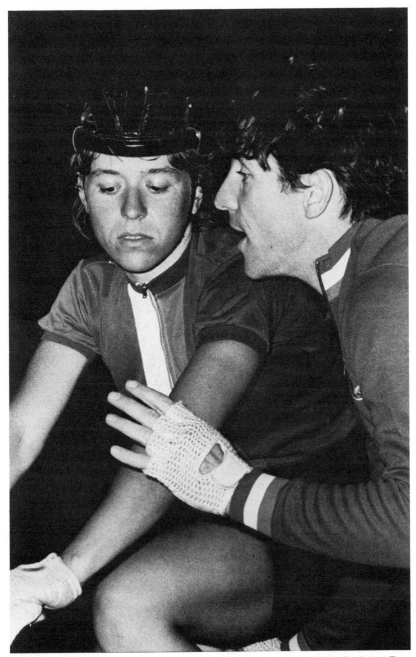

Reoch getting advice from racer John Chapman prior to a Match Sprint at Trexlertown.

Actually, Reoch trains as much as many senior men racers. For that reason she is discouraged when, after riding hundreds of miles in training, she is forced to participate in a race that is 10 miles.

Reoch's meteoric rise to racing fame, highlighted by her Silver medal in the World Pursuit Championships, suggests that bike racing in America is still open enough to allow an outsider to reach the top. For her part she would like to see more women enter racing to help make the sport more aggressive and exciting. Contrary to what many racers think, Reoch believes natural ability is secondary to training and dedication. "Training is terribly important. But as Bill Koch, the cross-country skier who won a Silver medal in the 1976 Olympics, said, all competitors have reached close to the same level, and it is 95 percent mental at that point."

Breakthrough with Audrey McElmury

Audrey McElmury arrived in Brno, Czechoslovakia, with very little money. Unsponsored by any organization, unsupported by an organized team, she started the Woman's World Championship Road Race without the infrastructure of confidence-building aids such as *domestiques*, depth of equipment and assistance, and simple financial security. She was an American rider little known in her country and less known in Czechoslovakia. The year was 1969.

The history of bicycle racing is, among other things, a history of great rides, tremendous efforts like that of Eddy Merckx in the 1975 Tour de France. Crashing terribly and riding with a smashed cheekbone and a concussion that would have put most men in the hospital, Merckx went on to challenge the leaders. Audrey's ride in the Championship Road Race was a rare American effort on this order.

McElmury stood in the pouring rain among 40 other women from 16 countries waiting for the start of the race. Since she did not have any team to block for her at the front of the peloton, McElmury was given little chance of success. Nonetheless, with one lap remaining she went off the front, dissatisfied with the slow pace. Racing down a hill, she crashed, and watched the field pass. Bleeding from her fall, she remounted and gave chase, regaining contact. Attacking on the last hill, she broke away a second time to

Robert F. George

Miji Reoch "cornering" during the National Road Championships in Milwaukee, Wisconsin.

Robert F. George

Stella Bastianella in a grueling hill climb in Skillman, New Jersey.

win by over a minute. Hers was a ride not yet equalled by any contemporary male rider. She had won the only World Road Championship to be won by an American of either sex.

Not surprisingly, she received more attention in Europe than she did in America. Europeans understood and appreciated her ride. Accordingly, she was immediately engaged by the Italian team, to ride for them and eventually coach them. Returning to this country McElmury still found it difficult to obtain travel expenses even though she was a strong enough rider to hold her own on the criterium circuit with the best American men, usually finishing in the top ten in criterium competition.

McElmury was a whirlwind, a muscular breeze to change the tone and tempo of women's racing in America. Standing five-feet eight-inches, weighing 130 pounds, McElmury has been the morning star for Young, Novara, and Reoch. In a sense modern women's racing begins with her. And she is outspoken about her training and dedication to cycling. "I can tell you," she said, "that until recently I don't think any U.S. man has trained as hard as I do. I lifted heavy weights. I used to do squats with a 135-pound barbell even when I was pregnant."

Before winning the Road championship McElmury trained for eight years, 40 miles a day, six days a week, nine months of the year. She has been known to train by climbing the stairs with ankle weights. When in active competition, she was considered the strongest woman rider. She did very well against the men, as the following lines from *Sports Illustrated* indicate:

"Seventy-seven of the best American racers were entered— Audrey and 76 men. 'It should be a spectacular race,' she said beforehand. 'There are lots of bad right-angle corners.' The road was narrow, with room for perhaps 15 cyclists abreast, and as the race began the tightly packed swarm looked like one of those giant, mutilated Things from a 3:00 A.M. movie with a dozen pistonlike legs and a thousand eyes—motes of chrome flashing in the sun.

"Jockeying for position in the middle of the maelstrom was Audrey McElmury, body low, hair streaming back. 'I'd rather look like a girl than cut my hair,' she says, but even with a crew cut she would have stood out like a rose in a potato patch.

"Fifteen miles into the race a cyclist fell directly ahead of

Audrey. She grimaced, swerved sharply to avoid a collision, then continued without hesitation, years of barbell curls paying off. She sat with the pack now, back and head almost parallel to the ground, face slightly upturned to reveal a tight-lipped mouth and the whites of her eyes. Rounding the next corner someone lost control and went down with a lingering clatter just behind Audrey. She curbed a dangerous reflex to look back.

"All went well until the next to the last lap. Going 35 mph, a cyclist trying to pass slapped his front wheel into Audrey's rear wheel, and suddenly three men were sprawled on the road. Again Audrey stayed upright, well-trained triceps, shoulders, and back resisting sudden lateral movement.

" 'She rides like a man, so why knock it,' Fred Davis of Westminster, California, had said before the race, 'I've got no fear of Audrey running into me, though there's a whole lot of guys I've got to watch.' Davis finished well behind the leaders, and Audrey, so out of shape after the World's that she had considered staying home, beat 64 of America's best men to finish thirteenth, despite losing half-a-dozen places in a sprint down the last 300 yards."

Contrary to what is believed by many, McElmury feels that women are closer to men in cycling than in other sports. "It is absolutely true," she said. "That's the reason we can compete with them. And because it is partly mental, which means tactics, we can compete with them. Obviously we can't compete with men in a time trial or a pursuit, because those races are just speed. But we can compete in endurance races. For example, in a criterium I have gotten in the top 10 because I knew what to do. I remember beating Bill Kund and a lot of people who were really good, just because I got in the right place and knew what to do. It had nothing to do with speed. I always used to get in the top 10 in criteriums just because I'd be in the right spot. I think road is better for women than track because they are endurance athletes."

McElmury acknowledges that many women riders and racers have a problem because "they can't get a bike that really fits them. Most women, compared to men, have short arms in proportion to their legs. So that's a problem. They look funny on bikes because they usually get stretched out. I have to have my bikes made shorter on the top tube."

Robert F. George

Miji Reoch and other women racers waiting for the start of a Road race in Tybee Island, Georgia.

Even so, McElmury feels that women are natural at cycling. She didn't change her mind when she gave birth to a son. "I didn't have any problems after having a child," she said. "In fact, I got about twice as strong. I set a whole bunch of records. They've written books about women athletes getting a lot stronger after they had children. They haven't proven anything. I know the year after I was pregnant I had the best year I ever had."

Having been the first American in many years to take a world title in Europe, McElmury's orientation is definitely European, with emphasis on motor-pacing, weight lifing, and hard riding. She believes cycling will become popular only after it becomes more of a spectator sport. At the present she feels the reason for the differences in success between Americans, especially the men, and Europeans is based on national character. "The reason that a lot of people in Europe get good at bike racing," she explained, "is because they don't have a chance to be anything but possibly a laborer. They will try a lot harder than someone here. They will sacrifice everything for it.

"A lot of the American riders don't have the same motivation that the European racers have. There is difference between fear of never making any money and the fear of never being anything. In Europe it is a question of survival. I knew the Italian Motor-pace champion. His side job was digging graves. That's what he would be doing full-time if he wasn't racing.

"Have you noticed the racers who have lost the World's, or did poorly, or had flats? The expressions? You see men crying because they count on it so much. You never see the American doing that."

CHAPTER FIVE

Families on the Road

JAMES C. MCCULLAGH

THE National Road Championships are proclaimed by a stiff banner strung across the windy highway which traces Milwaukee's luxurious lakeshore. Two American flags, one on each side of the banner, snap briskly, like yacht sails suddenly catching the wind. The road is deserted.

Every year, thousands of cyclists, mechanics, trainers, coaches, relatives, friends, and officials travel to a different section of the country to determine the nation's best road riders. Cycling officials spend the winter scouring the country for a road course that will test the speed, endurance, and bike handling of the riders. The Milwaukee road course promises to send more than one rider into early retirement.

Contestants come from most states, usually by car or van stuffed with bikes, sprockets, spare wheels, and food. Those who work often take their vacation for the event. Many drive all night to make the races. Some have been on the lakeshore for a week, whipping their bodies into final form in anticipation of the competition they did not get at home.

Home is hundreds of miles away for the majority of the participants who will test the road that seems to dip majestically to the lake. Home is where the racers qualified for the high summer event.

Even in the early morning the sun is merciless with its heat. The wind, stilled by the temperature, is now as negligible as the light mist that rapidly leaves the surface of the water. The banner is limp, almost wet. Men and women roll out of cars, trailers, and college dormitories on the hill to eat and check their machines. The road, already closed to traffic, is dotted with racers testing their legs after a long drive or a fitful night in the car.

They are joined by pleasure riders who want to take a piece of the course before the experienced racers put all the roadway before the wheel. The road opens in all directions as men and women pedal away their fears.

There is little of the carnival so often associated with sports. The banners and the flags pale behind the clusters of riders and confidants huddled to discuss tactics and the latest racing gossip. No cheerleaders, no marching bands; just hundreds of racers of all ages who assault the course with their machines.

The contestants are obvious, as they wear the bright colors of their club or sponsor. Less obvious at first glance is the skill of even the youngest racer who seems to mount his bike, adjust the pedal straps, and be off in a sprint in one long, graceful, motion.

All get their chance at cracking the course: the midgets, the juniors, the intermediates, the women, the veterans, and senior men. By noon the women have challenged the course. Now the attention is on the senior men, 18 to 40 years of age.

Two hundred riders stand in ranks across the lakeshore drive waiting for the gun. Ahead of them is a 123-mile, 28-lap race, which will take them initially through a lazy residential district above the lake, down a sharp S-curve to the shore front, before a long steady climb into the richly shaded hills. The final sprint will be straight and flat along the sun-scorched shore.

The ranks of men straddle their machines in the incandescent heat. Some are strangers on the national circuit, having earned the right to compete by winning their state championship. A rider from Pennsylvania conducts a last-minute survey of his friends to get someone to hand him water and juice at the "feeding" stations. Newcomers eye the seasoned racers, the favorites: John Allis, John Howard, Wayne Stetina.

Officials give directions and check the helmets of the men. The start-line crowd surges against the temporary picket fence. The gun sounds and the mass of riders jostle for position. Immediately, a local favorite shoots to the front and breaks away from the pack, causing restless chatter in the main body of riders. The pack is more content when it learns the one-man break has ended after the first lap.

Refusing the use of the wide Milwaukee lanes, the riders group together, forming a peloton where the riders tuck in behind each other getting relief from the torrid pace. The peloton, tidy and governable on the flats, strings out like an accordion on the hills. The accordion disintegrates into a shifting, dangerous pack line as the racers plunge down the S-curve and into a 90-degree turn on the asphalt waterfront. The turn takes many casualties.

Some of the more reckless riders, the crowd-pleasers, break away from the main body gaining vital seconds on their rivals only to be brought in by the aggressive riding of the pack. By the eleventh lap, however, a strong breakaway group gains a minute and a half on the rest of the riders, forcing a number to leave the peloton to join the chase. Racers at the front take turns pulling the other cyclists along the asphalt beach. The favorites remain in the pack.

A rider from California cries out for fruit juice as he passes the "feeding" area. A friend laterals a plastic bottle to the cyclist but misses. The rider curses and sprints to catch the riders who have passed him.

Halfway through the race Roy Stetina informs his sons, Wayne and Dale, that they are nearly two minutes behind the breakaway group. With only 75 racers left in the contest, the Stetinas make their move. Their chase group, regularly changing pace, attacks mercilessly, linking up with the "break" in 15 miles. Wayne Stetina splits the peloton and initiates a break. Pulling hard on his pedals, he punctures. A slow wheel change leaves him minutes behind the pack.

The lakeshore is at its hottest, close to 100 degrees F. The wind is dead. Sailboats stand idly in the water. Spectators seek refuge beneath their newspapers or trees. The heat escaping from the roadway is refracted in the bright sun. The lake is glass.

Long minutes behind the pack, Wayne pulls at his machine in the isolation of the open road. The bike sways as he stands in the pedals passing the stragglers. There is no peloton to ride with, no

Robert F. George

Robert F. George

Three cyclists break away from the peloton which remains tightly packed in spite of the climb.

John Howard, winner of the 1975 Senior National Road Championships.

Robert F. George

Feeding a rider in the "pit" area.

Troy Stetina in National Championship jersey.

A rider cools himself off after racin over a hundred miles.

The tip of the peloton. Riders "sit-in" behind the leader to conserve strength.

Robert F. George

Bike racing can involve the family and community, as it does in Kenosha, Wisconsin.

Robert F. George

Amateur riders "warm up" at the Kenosha, Wisconsin track.

rider to sit-in with on the Sahara straights. He attacks for a dozen blistering miles until he catches the pack, only to find Howard attacking in the hills, stringing out riders along the desperate accordion. Wayne abandons the chase after a few miles. Dale stays with the leaders to come in twelfth. Howard, strong and sinewy, wins. Three thousand delirious spectators surge against the fence, acknowledging Howard's victory salute.

Under the same Milwaukee sun, but earlier, Roy and Janice Stetina pace nervously within a throng of family and friends, surrounded by the spare wheels, the race-savers for the competitor. Roy speaks commandingly to Troy, his youngest son, about what gear he should use on the hills. Janice chats about the diet and training which have helped her sons become top athletes.

Both parents know that Troy, because of his name, will be a marked man. Most of all his parents are worried about spills. His father gives him simple advice: attack on the hills and be first down the slopes on the 10-mile course.

As Troy fights the 40-man field, his parents shower him with encouragement, tactics, and advice. The family chants in unison. Roy pierces the family call by reminding Troy not to spin in such a low gear. Troy responds and wins the National Championship jersey, which is as valuable to the clan as Olympic gold.

The tale of the National Chapionships is the tale of the jersey, the starred and striped symbol of excellence. And the jersey and its promises are what the Stetinas chase. Milwaukee is good to them.

Their first jersey was won by Wayne in the Time Trial Championship, accurately called the racer's test of truth. Through a gusting crosswind, over the undulating terrain of Port Washington, Wisconsin, Wayne chases the clock for 25 miles, beating John Howard by 46/100th of a second.

The National Championship banner is folded for another year. Many of the contestants return home and pack away their bikes. But not the Stetinas. They live to race and race to live.

Racing Families

American cycling history is, in some respects, the story of families who have made it to the top in the sport. The Butler brothers of the 1890s, the Walthours who raced during the first three decades of this century, and the Simeses and the Youngs of more recent fame, represent families who have given much of their energies to bike racing.

American cycling history is also the story of riders such as Frank Kramer and Major Taylor who believed in the axiom that superior health and training results in superior racing. Both lived simply, raced hard, and became world champions. These two greats represent the ultimate in the total discipline of mind and body.

For the last 40 years, racing in America has been a family sport in the best sense of the word. Parents sacrificed time and money to get their children to bike races in the next town or state. Olympic medalist Sheila Young has remarked a number of times that it was the dedication and unselfishness of her father that helped her along the way to great success in cycling and skating.

Jack Simes recalls the careful attention and advice his father gave him during his early years in racing. "Back in the 1950s there was really very little interest in racing, except for the people who had stayed with the sport. What I mean is, a kid couldn't get involved in the sport through television, as the kids do today with hockey and football. Rarely could you find information about cycling in the papers. You had to get the information somewhere, and it was usually from your father or relative with an interest in racing."

"I remember," Simes added, "all the time my father spent with me, teaching me about racing. He taught me how to balance, how to sit-in, how to come off a wheel, how to sprint. I couldn't get this kind of information anywhere else."

Entire families turning to bicycle racing for sport and recreation is not new. But rarely has a family as a unit been so dedicated to winning races and to general health as the Stetinas of Indianapolis. Although they have some distance to go to equal the successes of the earlier racing families, they have the potential to make a real contribution to American and world cycling. Regarded by many as the first family of cycling, the Stetinas have overcome health problems to excel at racing. In fact, they regard bike racing as an important part of their radiant good health.

Perhaps the best-known racing family in America, the Stetinas

Midget riders, ages 8 to 11, prepare to contest a heat at the National Road Championships.

have finished first or second against nearly impossible odds in many of the nation's most prestigious races. Four of the brothers race. The oldest, Wayne and Dale, travel the country together and win three-quarters of their races. Their father Roy is their coach.

Wayne and Dale spearhead a new movement among the amateur ranks of racers in America. Buoyed by their many victories, they are giving over more and more of their time to racing and training. They usually enter some of the early races in Florida, and then travel north to compete in the Somerville, New Jersey classic, then follow the racing circuit to other events in the Northeast, Midwest and West. As bike racing grows in popularity, they are discovering that it can be a full-time occupation.

The road of the amateur racer is difficult. Although the prize lists are improving, racing as an amateur, if done frequently, means giving up a lot of things in life. To devote their full energies to racing, the Stetinas have postponed their college studies. They are determined to be the country's best. Although the brothers have been on the racing circuit for only a few years, they have already written a number of chapters in their Cinderella story.

From Ill-Health to Championships

Roy, an ex-Ohio skating champion, discovered bicycle racing almost by accident, learning that skaters trained on bikes in the off-season. But it was after he attended a Six-Day bike race in the Cleveland Arena that he knew he wanted to race. He also had the good fortune to meet Torchy Pedem, one of the greatest Six-Day riders America has ever known. Stetina recalls that "Torchy and I trained together in Ohio on a beautiful 28-mile loop that we called the Brazilian Alps. We rode the course on a fixed-gear bike (without brakes) which allowed much closer riding than the freewheel bike with gears."

Stetina also recalls when he and his wife were riding competitively in Ohio. "A husband and wife riding competitively," he remarked, "was and still is unusual. People used to ask if we were brother and sister as we won the Ohio State Championship for several years in a row."

Janice's parents had restricted her physical activity because she had a heart murmur and they feared she might drop dead from a heart attack. "But outdoor exercise with friends in the fresh air and sunshine is just what I needed," she said.

In spite of their successes, the Stetinas were a very sickly family, whose frailty became more pronounced when the children were born. "All of us," Janice reported, "fell victim to poison ivy, rashes, colds, allergies, asthma, and other illnesses. Roy was constantly being leveled by allergies. Wayne and Dale succumbed to colds and flu and every childhood disease. During the hay fever season Dale had to walk around the house with an ice pack over his eyes to calm the itching and prevent swelling. Dale also had a sinus condition that lasted nearly every day of the year. We were fit for nothing, not for athletics, not for anything."

According to Janice, about this time a friend talked to her about the family's eating habits, which included using most of the store-bought products. Then she talked to Janice about "natural food and even showed me how to bake a loaf of whole grain bread. Well, since we thought we were eating a proper diet, I didn't take much notice. But, over a period of months and years, we ate low on the food chain—grains, fresh vegetables, sprouts, nuts, and seeds. All of us responded noticeably to better nutrition. The entire pattern of illnesses changed. Asthma attacks and tonsillitis, previously insurmountable problems, could be completely controlled. We noticed that the right food could help shrink swollen tonsils. Soon the boys were ready for athletics."

Wayne and Dale in particular made remarkable recoveries and became very successful at track and cross-country running but preferred the bike. Wayne progressed so rapidly that he made the Olympic cycling team in 1972. In the last few years he has won more than half the road races and criteriums that he has entered, usually averaging 10,000 miles a year in training. Dale has also experienced phenomenal success, being the youngest rider on a 1975 Pan-American cycling team.

As seniors, Wayne and Dale dominate much of the country's racing. Other competitors grumble whenever the "Ark" shows up. Over 40 feet long, the "Ark" is a traveling motor home used by the Stetinas for race transportation. It sleeps nine, travels a thousand miles on a tank of fuel, and has a refrigerator, stove, and a bathtub which is used for storing fruits and vegetables. All bicycles remain intact and are stacked on two levels. The wheel rack can accommodate an additional 30 spare wheels. Such a selection is needed because the racing circuit includes road races, criteriums, time trials, and track events, and different wheels are needed for each.

Although the major clubs in America organize racing teams for senior events, the Stetina-Stetina combination of Wayne and Dale is probably the closest and best working. People often ask the brothers how they get along while competing with each other all year. Surprisingly, there is very little quarreling. The brothers need each other to get back to the pack whenever they lose time to mechanical problems, to counter the tactics of the other teams, and to "work over" those riders who attempt to stay with the peloton without working and then win in the final sprint.

The brothers go out of their way to help each other. In a prestigious criterium in Florida, Wayne punctured, and lost minutes

Robert F. George

More and more riders are becoming conscious of their diets.

Robert F. George

Wayne Stetina showing a classic racing position during a Criterium in Hartford, Connecticut.

Robert F. George   Robert F. George

Dale and Wayne after winning the 50-mile race in Fitchburg, Massachusetts.

Dale Stetina racing against the clock at the Dorais velodrome in Detroit, Michigan.

Robert F. George   Robert F. George

Wayne Stetina in the four-man Team Time Trial at the World Championships in Montreal, Canada (1974). The U.S. team was ninth in the competition. Riders left to right are: Jim Ochowicz, Rich Hammen, Wayne Stetina, and John Howard.

Troy Stetina sprinting at the Northbrook, Illinois velodrome.

on the main body. Rather than staying with the rest of the pack, Dale went back to "pick up" his brother and help him regain the front. Taking turns setting the pace, the brothers eventually caught up with the peloton. Wayne was first, Dale second.

Both Wayne and Dale are excellent cornerers and bike handlers, so they enjoy racing in large packs. They both like hard, fast races common to Europe. "In Europe," Wayne explains, "there are more good riders, so packs generally move faster. Also, more races are available. In many countries a rider can race any day he wants within a 60-mile radius." Both find the prospects of racing in Europe enticing because the top European amateurs are well taken care of, fed, clothed, and housed, much as professionals.

Because Wayne and Dale each race over 50 times a year, a large part of their training is racing. They do not follow any set training schedule. Each day they determine what they need and do it. They ride anywhere from 200 to 500 miles a week depending on the season, the type of event they are training for, and how they feel.

The Stetinas try to ride as a group during training, not viewing their training companions as competitors. When the brothers get too far ahead, they turn back and regroup. Therefore, the beginning rider is not left behind to plod alone hopelessly. He is given the opportunity to keep up with the rest.

The Stetina family lives and breathes racing. With four boys involved in the sport, the parents give all their time and energies to help their sons succeed. The mother is an enthusiastic caretaker of their diets, the father of their racing tactics. They feel they have champions on their hands.

CHAPTER SIX

The European Scene

OWEN MULHOLLAND

EVERY international poll for the last several years has confirmed that the world's most popular sportsman is not Mark Spitz, Emerson Fittipaldi, Muhammad Ali or even the famous soccer player, Péle, but rather a Belgian bicycle racer named Eddy Merckx. Americans are often surprised to discover that a man they never heard of enjoys such reknown, but if present trends continue, the fascinating competition of professional cycling will not remain a mystery here in the United States much longer.

The thousands of North Americans in personal attendance at the World Cycling Championships at Montreal in 1974, and millions more who watched on television, were treated to a wonderful exhibition of just what professional road racing is all about when Eddy Merckx brilliantly won the 186-mile road race in just under seven hours of thrilling two-wheeled combat.

Yet the initial impact of seeing a hundred racers going at unbelievable speeds for an amazing length of time is but the first level of enjoyment, for this sport is one of the most complex games ever devised.

In winning this race Eddy Merckx not only gave a great display of his talents, but also wrote yet another chapter in the book of his own legend, a book which in turn is a chapter in the larger book of the history of cycling competition.

However magnificent his victory was, it becomes even more magnificent when it is realized that this is his third world cham-

Eddy Merckx (on right) surrounded by other Belgian riders during the World Championship Professional Road Race in Montreal, Canada (1974).

pionship, and that this feat has been accomplished by only two other riders in the entire 48-year history of these world title races.

This dimension of time, of history, perhaps one might almost say of mythology, gives the best racers an almost superhuman aura, particularly when one comes to understand the astounding nature of their efforts.

If the relentless speed over no less than 10,000 feet of climbs at Montreal amazed spectators new to the sport, what might they think if they could see these same men performing the same feat day after day for a full three weeks in a race such as the Tour de France? And what might they think if they could look back 40 or 50 years to the days when the Tour de France was contested by men with single-geared machines over unpaved roads for stages averaging double the current 150-mile daily stint?

The conclusion is inescapable that here is more than just another contest of a special skill. In its ultimate form, European professional bicycle racing brings men, at least a select few, to the very limits of human possibility.

Robert F. George

Mount Royal climb at the World Professional Championship Road Race, Montreal, Canada (1974).

The Making of a Classic

From the very beginning bike racing strived for the grandiose. Although there is still some debate, modern road racing generally traces its origin to the race from Paris to Rouen on the seventh of November, 1869.

Of course there had been some races before this time, enough even to prompt the publication of no less than two magazines devoted exclusively to this sport in France alone. It was one of these, *Le Vélocipède Illustré*, that announced on September 30, 1869:

"In order to further the good cause of the bicycle it must be demonstrated that the bicycle can be raced over considerable distances with incomparably less fatigue than running. By seeing for itself the public will be able to appreciate the real merit of the bicycle which makes a maximum economy of time and energy. Therefore, we announce a place-to-place race from Paris to Rouen, a distance of about 130 kilometers." Later editions printed more details and invited "all the racers of France and foreign countries to take part."

No less than 203 intrepid *"coureurs"* answered the call. The vast majority were French, of course, but there were some important exceptions: six English racers, three Belgian, and one German. Not to be overlooked were the entries of six women, including one who billed herself as "Miss America," although in reality she was British.

All contestants were required to sign in at 7:00 A.M. at the Place de l' Étoile before going on to the Arc de Triomphe for the official start at 8:30. A considerable number of the riders began to ride away to the Arc at 7:15, and the public, thinking that the race was on, sent up a great cheer. This, in turn, confused the riders. All it took was for a few to panic and the rest accelerated too, scared that they might be left behind. Through the Arc de Triomphe they shot, heedless of the cries to stop, and the race was on.

This left a number of others back at the sign-in, more than a little agitated at having missed the start. The officials managed to restore some semblance of order, and on the spot decided to give a second official start at 7:45 A.M. one half hour after the first, and the finishing order in Rouen would be adjusted to credit those who started later with the time difference.

Some of them didn't need it, however, and already by the second *"contrôle"* (sign-in points along the route to prevent riders from taking short cuts or the train) at 48 kilometers, three of the first ten came from the second group. "Miss America" arrived 1 hour 55 minutes after the leader, but that was still in fortieth place, or thirtieth if one credits her half-hour handicap!

A journal of the day reports that Miss America was cheered with unanimous acclamation as she passed. The small blond woman had extraordinary energy. She arrived at the *contrôle* with a calm and regular style, showing just a bit more color in her cheeks than normal as a sign of her efforts. She continued without wanting to stop.

A man on a horse who came close behind Miss America was reproached for riding so closely, but merrily he replied, "Who, me? But I've always chased women!"

Such bright sparks of amusement faded against the dark background of night which enveloped the riders. It was all the more menacing due to the inevitable fatigue and a fine rain that began to fall.

Since the beginning of the race the second rider on the road had been the Englishman, Johnson, but toward evening he became a pedaling automaton, carrying on without seeing or hearing. Finally, he fell against a fence where helpful spectators lifted him from his bike, carried him to a nearby house, and revived him with hot wine and food. Naively, Johnson had eaten only two sandwiches all day. Refreshed, he sallied forth again, now in fifth place. This scene was repeated over and over as rider after rider reached his limits, most often without the miraculous recuperation of Johnson.

In the end, only 33 of the original 203 arrived in Rouen, and most of these came in during the night. The British rider James Moore, riding with metronome regularity passed through the whole field to cover the 123 kilometers in 10 hours 40 minutes, a speed of about eight mph. Moore crossed the finishline at 6:10 P.M., but it wasn't until 6:20 A.M. that Miss America arrived, number 29, to claim the special prize for women.

The "disease" of bicycle racing proved to be as contagious as any epidemic of past epochs. Moore returned to England where he won a number of races. Italy, now also in the grips of bicyclemania, recorded its first race, Florence to Pistoia. Although the distance of 35 kilometers hardly qualified the race for enshrinement as a classic, it is of particular interest to Americans since one of our countrymen, with a rather un-American sounding name, Rynner Van Neste, then only 17 years of age, won the race in 2 hours 12 minutes over 32 other contestants.

The greater speed possible on the new "safety" bicycles tickled the fertile imagination of the various promoters, most of whom were attached to some cycling publication. The first of the great new races was Bordeaux to Paris, no less than 572 kilometers!

Presse Sports

Charles Terront. On this monster he rode the 120 kilometers of the Paris-Brest-Paris race in 1891, one of his many great feats of endurance.

To increase the speed, riders were to have pacers stationed along the way, a feature that has become characteristic up to the present day, although now the pacers are on small motorcycles.

Charles Terront, the French marvel, was not allowed to participate, since he, along with most of the best French riders, was a professional, and the British riders who had been invited insisted on amateurs only competing. The British swept the first three places, making their hosts regret their cooperation.

The 7,000 spectators who gathered to see the end of Bordeaux-Paris convinced the editor of the "*Petit Journal*" in Paris that such colossal races had a lot to offer in terms of publicity value. Unrestrained by the feat of having to undergo the ordeal himself, Pierre Giffard proposed a nonstop race from Paris to Brest and back to Paris, a distance of almost 800 miles, and this entirely on wretched country roads.

Giffard was accused of having gone too far, of creating such a monster that no riders would come, but he responded to all such forecasts of doom with a typical Gallic shrug, so sure was he of the insipient insanity even then characteristic of cyclists. His confidence was rewarded by almost 600 entries, 206 of whom actually showed up on the Sunday morning of September 6, 1891. Most prominent because he was clearly the popular favorite was "Le Grand Charles" (Terront, of course), who this time was unimpeded by rules regarding amateurism.

The British, already displaying the attitude that would soon remove them from the front seat of international cycling, declined to compete against those who made their livelihood from cycling. For them, sport was a class activity, open only to those who had the wealth and leisure time to indulge in hard work as play. The rift between professionals and amateurs on the continent was never allowed to expand to such proportions as to hurt the growth of the sport. The difference remained one of numbers and quality, not kind.

Whether or not the British could have halted Terront in the first Paris-Brest-Paris race is, in any event, improbable. He had already proved his unique abilities in this sort of marathon event on many other occasions and his performance over the farm roads west of Paris left no doubt in the minds of all observers that he was indeed the very best. Even his English pacer, Herbert Duncan, told him at the start that he was "better than the strongest of his adversaries," even those who might not have shown up.

His winning average speed of 17.6 kilometers per hour may seem pitifully slow by today's standards, but under the conditions it was close to the limit of human capabilities. I say "close," because although Terront undoubtedly rests as one of the greatest racers of all time, his progress was so impeded by a variety of delaying incidents that he could have finished much earlier.

As it was, he had a comfortable seven-hour forty-minute margin on his principal rival, Jiel Laval, when he pedaled at the beginning of the fourth day up to the finish line in Paris at 6:25 A.M., September 9. The phenomenal Charles had not had such a comfortable margin most of the way. Time after time he would gain a lead only to see it disappear after a flat, a broken chain, or, in one case, a search for the man at the control point who had wandered off in search of a warm place to sleep. In fact, Laval had preceded Terront by 40 minutes to the turnaround at Brest.

The mighty Charles took only six minutes to refresh himself in Brest after 35 nonstop hours in the saddle. He protested to reporters that "without these flats I would have been ahead by an hour. But if I can pedal regularly I will catch him before Paris."

But the gap was to grow even wider, thanks to yet more mishaps, before the balance of luck swung the other way and Laval was forced to seek a few hours sleep in the little town of Guingamp. By coincidence this was also a town in which Terront had passed some of his military service, so upon learning that Laval was catching a few winks, Terront took back streets which he could navigate in the dark thanks to his memory, and passed out of the town without Laval or his attendants being any the wiser.

When Laval arose and demanded of his doorman if Terront had passed and was assured of the negative, he even permitted himself the luxury of a bit more sleep. Only later did he discover that Terront had a four-hour lead, one which now only increased.

Up to the Porte Maillot in Paris, Charles Terront rode his way into legend amidst the ecstatic cheers of 10,000 persons. So formidable was his accomplishment that 10 years passed before the race was revived. The 10-year interval was maintained up to

Gaston Rivière, winner of the Bordeaux-Paris race in 1897 and 1898.

modern times. Since then the "race" has been organized more frequently, but only for tourists whose mania for masochism of a certain type exceeds even that of the pros.

Paris-Brest-Paris and Bordeaux-Paris remained the two super classics, but other races of slightly more humane dimensions were started in this era and have continued down to the present day as the high points of the professional calendar. In France, Paris-Roubaix and Paris-Tours were both begun in 1896. Belgium joined the club in 1892 with Liège-Bastogne-Liège, Paris-Brussels in 1893, and in 1913 the Tour of Flanders. Italy moved into the elite world of classics a few years later by introducing the Tour of Lombardy in 1905, and then Milan-San Remo in 1907.

Luc Lesna (France) poses with his flowers after winning Paris-Roubaix in 1901. He covered the 260 kilometers in 10 hours 49 minutes. He was the winner of the same race the following year.

Most of these races didn't begin as classics. They were just several of many others, but over the years they rose to a special position because of the prizes, their difficulties, their popularity, and the quality of the participants. Only three races have been added to this very special list since World War I: Belgium's Flèche Wallone (1936), Germany's Henninger Turm (1962), and Holland's Amstel Gold race (1966).

All these classics are intimidating enough, even in modern times with our good roads, light bikes, and fast replacement service for mechanical breakdowns. They average about 180 miles in distance and only one is even reasonably flat. Each has its own character, its particular combination of roads, crowds, time of year, hills, and weather. Most require at least seven hours of unimaginable labor to complete.

However difficult things seem to be today, they were even harder back in the beginning. Consider the bicycle that Terront cajoled from Paris to Brest and back. It was a 40-pound machine with an enclosed chain. Top tube and down tube did their best to be parallel, so Charles sat pretty well upright. There was little in the way of special clothing—without toe clips and straps Terront had no need for any shoes other than those he normally wore in the street. Braking was operated by a system of metal rods that ultimately pressed a metal spoon directly onto the front tire. (No wonder he had so many flats!). Not that the tires were insubstantial.

The roads left more than a little to be desired. All the old pictures show these stalwart racers loaded down like so many wandering sausage salesmen, with extra tires wrapped across their backs and shoulders and strapped under the saddles. The combination of adversities reduced the race speeds to snail-like proportions. Yet very early the public grasped what an astounding feat 20 kilometers per hour for 400 kilometers was under these conditions.

For the first Paris-Brussels, 30,000 Parisians turned out just as darkness fell, to see the contestants pedal off into the night on the 407-kilometer odyssey. Some of the racers had more adventure than they anticipated, becoming completely lost, but 19 hours and 40 minutes later, an equally grand reception awaited the winner, Andre, upon his entry into the velodrome at Brussels. Only the King had had to leave before Andre's arrival, and that slight was corrected with an official audience a few days later. (In fact, such a convert was the King that he bought a tricycle the next year and went training every morning, and this when in his sixties!)

The Tour de France

By the turn of the century the sport was well established. One must recall that the myriad diversions to which the modern public is subjected were not available then. No television, no radio, no car, no movies—just the daily toil, the local bar, and a weekend at the town gardens or bicycle track. All the pent-up passions of a hard week were displaced onto the riders, come the weekend. Into this confined little world the daily newspaper brought virtually the only fresh information about happenings elsewhere. Each paper had its faithful following, prepared to defend its editors' pronouncements in extremely vociferous style if need be.

What applied to the normal publications applied to the cycling papers even more. The ultimate example must be the bitter feud between Pierre Gliffard, now of *"Le Vélo,"* and Henri Desgrange of *"L'Auto,"* subtitled, *"Automobile - Cyclisme."*

For example, after *"Le Vélo"* had organized the Bordeaux-Paris race on May 30, 1902, as it had the 11 previous such races, Desgrange organized another in the same year on August 24. The first race was won by the modest rider, Watelier, while Desgrange's race was won by the famous Maurice Garin. On the other hand, the latter's time was inferior to that of the former. You may be sure that these and many other such points did not go unnoticed by the respective journals.

But Desgrange wanted to stage a race of such magnitude that *"Le Vélo"* would be permanently relegated to second class status. He racked his brain for some idea, for something truly unique. One day, a co-worker proposed the idea of a six-day race; not on the track, but on the country roads around the whole of France! It was just the kind of crazy notion that Desgrange was looking for. Even with all the obvious obstacles, its appeal was so great that no one on the staff really opposed the idea, least of all Desgrange, who immediately went to work on the details.

By January 19, all was ready, and in banner headlines, *"L'Auto"* announced, " 'Le Tour de France'; the greatest bike race in the whole world. A race of more than one month: Paris - Lyon - Marseille - Toulouse - Bordeaux - Nantes - Paris. 20,000 francs in prizes. Departure - June 1, arrival - July 5 at the Parc des Princes track." Subsequently, the time was chopped down to 19 days, but the format was otherwise basically the same. Each day's 400 kilometer stage would be followed by several days of rest. The formula proved to be a great success. The race, which started with something less than the desired enthusiasm of the public, returned to Paris in triumph with its victor, Maurice Garin, hailed as a hero.

But Desgrange's troubles had just begun. If the first edition had established the race as something unique and marvelous, then the second edition showed what a victim of its own success the Tour had already become. As the race passed through the different regions, the locals naturally gave all possible verbal assistance to the home favorite. The assistance unfortunately degenerated into something more than verbal on the Col de la République near St. Etiènne, when the supporters of Faure threw the Italian, Gerbi, off his bike and onto the pavement with such force that he broke his finger. Only when the following cars arrived and guns were drawn did the melee break up.

Elsewhere around France, tacks were thrown on the road and routes were barricaded. This latter obstacle posed more difficulty than one might at first suppose. The stages generally started around 2:00 A.M. in order to arrive at the finish in daylight hours. Often the riders had to navigate through the murky night all alone and with no light. A felled tree usually wasn't obvious until rammed!

Desgrange was in despair, even writing in "L'Auto" at one point that "The Tour is finished; this second edition is the last . . ." It was, of course, too good to let die. For the following year Desgrange altered the course, adding more stages of slightly shorter duration which eliminated much of the night riding. This set the pattern, still used today, of altering the course from year to year. In 1905 he included the first mountain pass, and so pleased was he with this new torment for the riders that he placed three on the itinerary for 1906. With 4,637 kilometers to cover in this year, the Tour was more than ever an amazing cavalcade of incidents.

Against this background of near interminable distances, wretched roads, and cumbersome bikes, all those who completed the journey could be excused for feeling some pride in their achievement. Inevitably, there were dramas that made each race memorable.

Eugene Christophe, whose name is inscribed on the majority of toe clips these days, began an appalling sequence of undeserved Tour de France misadventures in 1913 when he broke his fork in

Maurice Garin, winner of the first Tour de France.

Eugene Christophe, hero of so many great and sad moments.

Fausto Coppi leads his Italian rival, Gino Bartali in the 1949 Tour de France. Both men were at the summit of the sport for nearly 20 years.

the Pyrenees. On this particularly mountainous stage he had moved into first place and was going all out, when (as he recounted in an interview many years later), "all of a sudden, about 10 kilometers from St. Marie de Campan down in the valley, I feel that something is wrong with my handlebar. I cannot steer my bike anymore. I pull on my brakes and stop. I see my fork is broken! I can tell you now that my fork was broken, but I would not tell you at that time because it was bad advertising for my firm.

"So there I was, left alone on the road. When I say the road, I should say the path. All the riders I had dropped during the climb soon caught me. I was weeping with anger.

"I was getting madder and madder. As I walked down I was looking for a short cut. I thought that maybe one of these steep pack trails would lead me straight to St. Marie de Campan. But I was crying so badly I couldn't see anything. With my bike on my shoulder, I walked for all those 10 kilometers.

"On arriving in the village I met a young girl who led me to the blacksmith on the other side of the village. M. Lecomte was the name of the blacksmith. He was a nice man and he wanted to help me, but he was not allowed to. The regulations were strict; I had to do all the repair by myself. I never spent a more wretched time in my life than these cruel hours in M. Lecomte's forge. Members of rival cycling firms had been sent to keep a close watch on me. M. Lecomte was only allowed to give me verbal guidance. A young boy helped me handling the bellows, for which aid I was fined. After three hours' repair I was able to continue on an uncertain and rather unsafe bike. I had lost the Tour de France."

World War I canceled out the lives and careers of a whole generation of cyclists. Christophe was one of the few to survive, and in 1919, when the Tour came back to life under the omnipresent guidance of Desgrange, Eugene was there, eager to at last win this race which should already have been his.

He had every reason to be hopeful, for by the time the race had arrived in Nice, two-thirds of the way through its loop around France, he was leading it. By coincidence, he became the first man to ever wear the now famous "*maillot jaune*," or yellow jersey. It was another of Desgrange's brainstorms, the color being easily visible to the crowds and also the color of "*L'Auto's*" pages.

Christophe carried on at the head of affairs, seemingly destined to at last win the race to which he had dedicated his life. But on the next to last stage (a little 468-kilometer jaunt from Metz to Dunkerque, if you please!) he once again had the misfortune of breaking his fork on the terrible roads of northern France, most of which still hadn't been repaired since the war. (Readers familiar with the cobblestone and potholed roads used in the present-day Paris-Roubaix race will agree that there has been no change in the last 60 years!) If you smell a forge blazing away in the next village your intuition is perfectly correct. This time he was delayed two hours and dropped from first to tenth place, or next to last, the 58 other starters having dropped by the wayside along the war-torn roads of Europe.

Christophe had his share of problems outside the Tour de France as well. For example, in the 1921 Paris-Brest-Paris he found himself isolated with four Belgians in the front group. With Paris 100 kilometers away they attacked in turn, but the old Frenchman wasn't dead yet. Letting one of them, Mottiat, gain a 13-minute lead, he jumped away from the others and began to pull back the difference.

Then Christophe flatted a tire. A spectator offered him a bike which he lumbered along on for a while, but it was poorly equipped so he changed it for another when the opportunity presented itself. Then a new flat tire. This time he had to repair it by hand. A little further on the chain broke. A second Belgian, Emile Masson, passed. Finding yet a third bike, Eugene once again resumed the pursuit as best he could with a wobbly rear wheel and two broken toe clips. Nevertheless, he was able to pull back on Masson and just 200 meters from the finish, he dashed by the Belgian to take second place!

Christophe was a forerunner of the present day Raymond Poulidor in the sense that both have risen to fame through almost-but-not-quite performances, performances that arouse tremendous sympathy among the fans. As recently as 1974, the beloved "Poupou" (Poulidor), then age 38 and the idol of all France, nearly pulled off the upset of all time when he dropped everyone, including one M. Eddy Merckx, during a Pyrenees stage of the Tour de France. It was a great ride which catapulted him into second place, but it was the last day in the mountains and therefore his last chance to win this race whose final victory had been almost his 14 times.

I don't mean to give the impression that professional cycling is nothing but a kaleidoscope of tragic heroes. Each generation has certainly produced its share of great champions as well.

King of the Road

But one need not look to history to find all the epic rides. The style has changed from an exercise in slow motion to one of quicker intensity, but the effort is still the same. In our own time one man dominates the sport as none other before him, and in so doing he has assembled a list of victories longer than anyone ever before. Eddy Merckx is the absolute quintessence of what a top professional cyclist should be. Aggression is his middle name. From March through October Merckx is at all the races, always giving of his very best no matter what his personal disposition may be.

Merckx came into the sport during the mid-sixties when a dull pattern was beginning to dominate the races. The top riders were so similar in ability that they tended to stalemate each other. In the 1968 Tour of Italy the Belgian man burst these patterns with his seemingly inexhaustable energy. Every day he could be seen at the front, battering away. Old hands who expected this brash fellow to collapse when the going got tough had to eat their words on the toughest day of all. The climb up The Tre Cime de Laverado is one of the most severe mountain pass climbs in Europe, even under normal circumstances. But in 1968 the normal circumstances were eliminated by a snow storm which turned the race into a crawling match. Only Merckx was able to navigate the drifts at anything like a respectable pace.

In the spring of 1969 he won no less than three classics, a feat virtually unheard of before, especially for a man who was supposed to be saving himself for the summertime Tour de France. All Belgium desperately wished for a win, inasmuch as it had been 30 years since a Belgian had last won the Tour.

But he proved himself ready enough when the time came. On the very first mountain he attacked with such ferocity that he rele-

Presse Sports

Merckx's team sets the pace at the front of the peloton during a stage in the Tour de France.

gated all the other pretenders to a 4 minute 21 second deficit. Two days later he won a time trial at a speed that would have made him world champion in the pursuit, and followed that up with more big time gains in the Alps.

With almost 10 minutes on the second man, 1967 Tour winner Roger Pingeon, Merckx was advised to rest a bit. Why should he set the pace? But on the big four-mountain stage in the Pyrenees, Merckx could contain himself no longer. Near the summit of the third climb he left his rivals standing, more to give himself some elbow room on the twisting descents than to really go for the stage win still over 100 kilometers distant, or so he later claimed. Be that as it may, at the bottom his lead had increased to a couple minutes, and without undue strain he proceeded over the last pass and on to the finish, gaining all the way along the final flattish kilometers where theoretically the madly chasing group behind should have had some advantage. In the end, he had nearly eight minutes lead over the second rider, so in one afternoon he had doubled the time gap on his nearest challenger, Pingeon. This was the day Merckx showed he had only himself to beat.

Pieter Van Damme

Even the greatest must suffer. Here Merckx pounds up a cobbled hill in obviously miserable condition. At least there is a large crowd to cheer him on.

In the succeeding years things haven't been quite so easy as the other riders have adapted to the new standard he has imposed. Yet even in the face of certain defeat, he fights on to his last drop of energy. The 1975 Tour de France is a good example. Not climbing quite as well as a few years ago, and with five mountaintop stage finishes on the itinerary, Merckx was at something of a disadvantage against the younger Bernard Thevenet who had been groomed almost exclusively for this event for several years. Yet despite a blow in the stomach from an irate fan, and later a crash

Merckx gets fast service from his team mechanics when he has a flat tire.

that broke a bone in his cheek, thereby forcing him onto an all-liquid diet, he never gave up, even attacking in the first kilometer of the last stage against hopeless odds. Immediately he began planning his revenge for this defeat and all followers of the sport around the world eagerly awaited a rematch.

If the bulk of this chapter has dealt with professional cycling on the road, it is because this is the most important feature of the modern sport. Early season races begin on the Riviera in February as preparation for the spring classics in Italy and northern Europe. Three big national Tours follow, those of Spain, Italy, and France, each about three weeks in length, and spaced through May, June, and July. By the time the Tours have finished the year's heroes have been well established, so August is dedicated to small invitational races around Europe where all the folks in the little towns can see the stars up close. The World Championships at the end of the month usher in a renewed period of prestigious classics that carry on to the middle of October, at which point the inclement weather sends at least some of the riders indoors to the winter board tracks.

Americans Abroad

Time was, of course, when the track was more than a series of wintertime Six-Day races. Victor Linart, one of the greats from the past (four times World champion and 15 times Belgian champion) spoke to this writer at the World Championships in Belgium during 1975. Attendance at the track was nothing like what he had known in his day. "As recently as 1958 we had 80,000 spectators at the track for the World's, now it is all finished. Here they care only for the road. It's the fault of the promoters who have let other sports advertise better and take public attention away from our sport.

"The biggest names in racing used to be on the track. Just imagine if they held the track races after the road races and had Eddy Merckx here to ride the pursuit; the place would be jammed."

M. Linart's specialty had been motor-paced racing, but he got into it almost by accident. "Like everybody else, I started on the road, but it was a pretty tough business in those days. If you punctured, and you punctured pretty often, there were no cars following with spare wheels. You had to change the tire yourself. No quick release gadgets, not even wing nuts.

"I was leading in a race by three minutes when the tire went bang. I finished three minutes back in eleventh place, and pretty fed up, because there were only prizes for the first ten.

"The race finished on a track where the great French motor-paced follower, Paul Guignard, was riding a match. When somebody told me he was being paid 3,000 francs appearance money— 10 times the first prize for the road race—I decided I wanted to be a motor-paced rider as well."

Certainly Victor went on to the greatest glories the sport has to offer, but just as interesting to me, as an American, was his infatuation with American racing during the early 1900s. He was racing in Germany when the war broke out, and not without a little luck he was able to make his way to England. From there he contacted the American track rider, Floyd MacFarland, and by return cable he soon had an invitation to the United States.

Upon arriving he found that "everybody was good to me, one rider lending me shorts, another shoes, somebody else a few jerseys, and Frank Kramer let me have two bikes. Then Floyd put me straight into a Six-Day race—and I hadn't been on the bike for three months!"

He survived, regained his form, and soon was riding on the myriad tracks sprinkled around the Northeast. As a motor-paced rider he could command $200 per race and compete several times a week. So strong was the pull of the American scene, that even after the war when he had returned to Europe, he came back once again in 1922.

That American scene is described in greater detail elsewhere in this book, and with considerable justification, for it was the Americans who became specialists on the small board tracks and taught the Europeans how to navigate around the near-vertical bankings.

Slowly the scene died out in America, almost completely extinguished by World War II. Prior to 1969, our last World champion had been Frank Kramer in 1912, the very same man who had lent Victor Linart his bikes. But he is remembered in Europe more for his victories over the French champion, Gabriel Poulain, in the Prix de Paris in 1905 and 1906. So unhappy were the Parisians with this second success that they pelted the American with everything they could lay their hands on. Today, however, he is still remembered in Europe as the most "complete" sprinter of the pre-World War I period. With perfect position and style he won races at every distance.

No doubt Kramer was individually brilliant, but he was pushed to his best by the hoard of other American sprinters nipping at his heels. He was, in fact, the third man in a succession of world champion sprinters produced on this side of the Atlantic.

The first had been Arthur Augustus Zimmerman, winner of the first World Championships ever held (1893, Chicago), and subsequently the absolute master of sprinting around the world for

Frank Kramer and Gabriel Poulain, before a Match Sprint in Paris, France during the early part of the nineteenth century.

nearly a decade. On his way to France in 1893 he collected the British championship, and then went on to his next race in Bordeaux. There he took the first match so easily that the officials approached him with a request to try something different to make it look better. He replied with a calm, "After the bell." Against three Frenchmen he occupied himself contentedly in last position for the first three of four laps. The lead man, Vogt, obviously meant to sacrifice himself for the others by setting a furious pace. The bell sounded, announcing the last lap, and still Zimmerman was apparently happy to follow in last position and seemed intent on staying there. But then, in the final turn, he emerged from the rear position like a rocket, passed the other three at a stupefying pace which gave them no chance to come back at him, and sailed on across the line 20 meters clear of the second man.

"Zimmy" with his trainer.

Cross comparisons between eras are always difficult, but by any standards, Zimmerman was one of the best ever. He recorded 12 seconds flat for the final 200 meters, a not embarrassing time today. When one realizes that this time was recorded in a rather upright position, on a bike weighing 26 pounds utilizing toe clips without straps, heavy tires, and a low gear, then one begins to appreciate what his phenomenal 160 revolutions per minute really meant. Obviously such a sprinter didn't accelerate by force, but rather progressively, like an electric motor!

But the Europeans felt confirmed in their suspicions that there was more than inborn ability to the feats of "Zimmy" when he described his training and racing schedule. Not only did he ride with others at high speeds for 10 miles every day, but he was able to race virtually as often as he wished. One year he won a bet by winning more than 100 races in a season! At the time, most track riders in Europe only raced on Sundays, and this revelation by the American helped to speed up the program over there.

Between Zimmerman and Kramer came a man unique in the annals of the sport. Not only was Major Taylor one of the rare black men to ever seriously race (a situation that is rapidly changing today), but he was also one of the most successful of any color. It is sad to notice that the dragnet thrown back through history by modern black historians in search of great black personalities has somehow completely slipped by this unforgettable figure.

He is remembered abroad in particular for his series of sensational matches with the French champion, Edmond Jacquelin. Incidentally, win or lose, Mr. Taylor was guaranteed no less than $7,500, a figure hard to estimate in today's inflated economy, but one which we can be assured is comfortably beyond whatever the current world sprint champion is able to command. In the end, he beat Jacquelin, two matches out of three, and so upset was Desgrange (yes, the father of the Tour de France), director of the track, that he paid Taylor in 10 centime pieces. This is indicative of the petty (and not so petty) annoyances that the man had to endure all through his life.

Those were the great days that American cyclists look back to with longing. Beginning in the 1960s a steady trickle of riders has gone to Europe to attempt to break into the ranks. Most have come back after a few years, overwhelmed by the speed of the racing, the expenses, the loneliness, and the language problems. The number of American men who have gone to Europe and failed is almost without end.

At present the problem is being attacked from two directions. First, a few of America's best amateurs, particularly track riders, have turned professional in the last few years. Jack Simes, John Vande Velde, and others were able to break into the wintertime Six-Day circuit. One of the most successful was Tim Mountford from Los Angeles who managed to sustain himself for several years through his racing efforts.

A second direction, not entirely inconsistent with the first, is the development of our amateur talent in depth. Many of these men have elected to stay in the United States and race abroad only on U.S. teams. That the home standard has increased impressively in the recent past is shown by American performances in the Tours of Ireland, England, and Canada. As recently as 1970 the thought that Americans could compete in such races was laughable. Now our racers are invited to participate.

Those who have journeyed to Europe to ride have been impressed by the glamour, the speed, and the demands of the sport. Jim Stillmaker, who spent two seasons in Europe to satisfy a dream, occasionally was obliged to ride a train to a race with his partially dismantled bike wrapped up in a cloth bag (to avoid paying a stiff surcharge for bicycles). In the changing room before a criterium in Holland he recalled that "all is subdued chaos. It's usually crowded and some of the tenser riders are laughing a little too hard. But for most, especially the trade team riders, it's business as usual. You can't help being a bit anxious but you have to stay as calm as possible. You'll need all your energy for the race. After dressing, 'oiling,' and a light massage you finish off whatever pre-race food you've prepared and put a few morsels of something in a jersey pocket. Just enough time for a couple of warm-up laps.

"If you're lucky, it isn't too cool yet and you ease around the course taking note of any unusual hazards. The race start itself is just as disorganized as U.S. races. Front row places go to those who get there first and those who push their way in later. Starting position can make a difference even in a 100 kilometer race—the standard distance for 'Amateur' riders. Some races are as short as 80 kilometers and a few are 110 or 120 but 90 percent are 100 kilometers. But this isn't an accurate measurement. The courses aren't surveyed and no claims for records are made. The newspapers record the winning time but it's only a formality.

"The 'rounds' are anywhere from 800 to 2000 meters in length but most fall in the 1000–1500 meter range. The officials are fond of 100 lap races regardless of the actual distance per lap. In spite of the bricks, wind, punctures, and hundreds of 90-degree corners, crashes are relatively rare except on some of the more absurdly acrobatic courses.

"There are only two classes of adult men recognized in Holland: '*Liefhebbers*,' first year, veteran, and family-men types who make themselves ineligible for that year's championship events by choosing to ride in this class—and 'Amateurs.' The 'Amateurs' have more races offered them each year than all the other classes, including Pros, put together.

"There's usually a long wait at the start while the officials get themselves straightened out. Dutch officials are more organized and business-like than most U.S. officials. They get more practice, I guess, but usually have some loose ends to tie. The race starts fast and gets progressively faster as the 100-man peloton snaps into a long snaking string. Weaker riders crack, lose contact, are quickly lapped and pulled from the race. All lapped riders are pulled to avoid confusion and possible collision between members of the same trade teams. The announced race distance is not sacred. If 10 or 15 riders lap the field the race jury may ring the bell (lap) for everyone else to sprint for the remainder of the place prizes.

"Fifty to eighty percent of most fields are composed of sponsored riders who receive bonuses for placing in the top five. Sometimes the bonus is greater than the prize and some "name" riders receive start money of more than $100. (That's why a lot of Dutch 'Amateurs' don't want to turn Pro.)

"Place prizes are awarded to twentieth place. Primes (special prizes for winning laps) are awarded almost immediately after the start but unless you're near the front at the start you can't get close enough to fight for one in the opening laps even though prime prizes are awarded for the first three to eight riders. Primes are

Pieter Van Damme   Pieter Van Damme

Ronald De Witte after the Paris-Roubaix race.

Professional riders racing in the rain in Belgium.

never listed in advance of the race. They are thrown in at the discretion of the promoters to keep spectator interest high.

"Although most riders carry some food and liquid there is little time to eat and drink. 'Drivers' ride with their hands on the drops all the way and everyone comes out of the corners sprinting for all they're worth. Dutch brick streets are built smoother than most Belgian brick roadways. The Dutch use smaller, flat-topped red bricks on most streets but have rougher grades of bricks too. The riders ease before the corners but don't brake—even on narrow streets.

"If the pace is easy the riders bunch at the corners and slide through locked, sometimes physically, shoulder to shoulder. Usually though, the pace is frantic and the string of riders sweeps the towns from gutter to gutter locked tightly to the wheel in front. It's a beautiful but dangerous ballet. When the pace really heats up the biggest challenge is to avoid hitting the far curb and still hold onto a wheel. The latest Dutch pop tunes are pumped out over a system of loudspeakers that ring the course and a professional announcer keeps riders and spectators informed of coming primes and announces the names of winners of previous primes.

"Madly spinning legs spring you out of each turn. You try to relax and let the effort flow the ra-ta-ta-ta-ta-bump-ta-ta-bump-bounce-bang of the bricks batters the body and brain in spite of deliberately half-deflated tires. The pace is killing but you try to move up to fight for primes knowing that the bulk of the money is given out there rather than to the survivors who get the prestige of winning. The race winner of a *schema one* race (place prizes are firmly legislated according to several grades of *schemas*. Most races are number ones—total place prizes equal approximately $320—but primes may total five times that) gets about $32. A first place prime is usually worth $10 (but sometimes merchandise is given for primes). Of course a race win might attract a sponsor who would provide race clothing and some equipment plus those bonuses for future top-five placings.

'Flashing inside' on corners, closing gaps left by weaker or punctured riders, you move up—often playing the fatiguing leap-frog games, passing and being passed by others with the same idea. If luck, legs, and lungs hold out you finally get to the front. Here are the aces. These are the guys you see in the glossy color photos in the continental racing magazines. And this is how they 'train' to win major tours like Britain's Milk Race.

"Attack! Attack!! Riders are firing away in every direction . . . on the left . . . on the right . . . attack! attack! . . . counter attack!! A small group moves a few precarious lengths clear and 'settles down' to an intense team pursuit effort.

"Singly and in twos and threes, riders from behind fire desperately up the road after them. Everyone wants to get into the break. No one but a 'silly foreigner' would think to organize the peloton to chase. Usually it makes no difference anyway as the break is absorbed as quickly as it was formed and the whole process is repeated again and again.

"Battered and aching your brain numbs and drifts off to never-never land. You've been living and dreaming cycling and now your legs spin by themselves and you sweep through corner after corner so dazed you're not sure whether it's just another dream or a living

Pieter Van Damme

This monument to Stan Ockers, one of the great Belgian riders of the 1950s, shows the veneration in which these sportsmen are held.

Start of the Veterans' National Championship Road Race in Milwaukee, Wisconsin (1975).

nightmare. The evening wears on and the cold wind stabs at fatigued legs that must respond to the last desperate efforts of riders trying to break free from the hard core of survivors.

"Somehow a small group always gets clear. Big bunch finishes are common but not for first prize. Occasionally the winner will flash across the finish alone, hands raised high in delighted disbelief. Most times it's a small handful that bob and weave into view on the bell lap. Silhouetted by the lights of the escort motorcycles, one rider jumps clear from the final, bouncing ballet of his companions and streaks on to the finishing straight with the others closing fast. At the line they're all side-by-side again but one man has won.

"On their heels come the rest. If it's a large group they jam the road from curb to curb and the last corner will be something you'll never forget. One man kicks out of the corner a fraction too soon and harmless yellow-orange sparks fly out into the night—someone has just lost another millimeter of pedal.

"Switching, slashing, and scrambling with a flair that the Three Musketeers never had, the big bunch scoops up the remaining place prizes.

"It's over! Tough men, cracked around the edges and drenched in sweat, ride off into the cold darkness while the equally fatigued but happy winner is swamped with flowers—and the eager crowd presses forward to see what a winner looks like.

"The changing room isn't so crowded now. Most of the men (the early casualties) have already come and gone again. The survivors move slowly now. Each man silently collects his thought and senses. It was so close. The winner is a good man—but it could have been any of them. They know that . . . You know it too.

"Road dirt swept up from cracks in the bricks coats fatigued limbs. Time to wash. Every muscle in your body aches. You don't just ride with your legs here."

Conclusion

The Return of Popular Cycling

"You'll never get me on that thing," cried a middle-aged man from Trexlertown, Pennsylvania, home of one of the nation's finest velodromes. The man's fear was aroused by the slope of the track, measured at 27 degrees. Reluctant to ride on the banking, he stood at the finish line, leaning on his road bike and watching a swarm of riders move around the oval. Some, as if guided by rope, hugged the pole line at the inside of the track. Others, lured by the banking, pedaled easily above the relief line, surprised that they could maintain their balance at such a crawl. Every few minutes a rider would swing cautiously to the top of the track, gaining his breath and letting his legs recover. On different plateaus, at different speeds, dozens of riders of all ages traveled around the saucer.

The man from Trexlertown observed the steady motion of men and machines. He heard the hum of the tires against the smooth, fast surface of the velodrome. He mounted his bike and moved slowly around the track apron, well clear of the other riders. Soon, he felt the pull of the track. Timidly, he joined the string of pacers at the pole line. Gaining speed, he tucked-in behind the other riders as if attached to a powerful towline. He had never ridden as close to other riders before; it was almost as if he could hear the wheels squeak.

Tired, but exhilarated, he dropped to the apron and dismounted. The circular whirr of the bikes on the banking no longer seemed so formidable. Sitting in the stands waiting for the races, he remarked; "A few months ago I wouldn't let my children near the track and I was dead scared of the thing. But, you know, it's easy. Anyone can ride a velodrome."

The above scene, startling to some and predictable to others, has been witnessed frequently at most of the velodromes in the country. At the opening of the East Point, Georgia track, a 10-year-old girl, unimpressed by the 33 degree slope, celebrated the event by calmly pedaling around the velodrome on her small bike. She was demonstrating what racers had always known: almost anyone can ride a velodrome.

Aerial view of night racing at Trexlertown.

If the ultimate in cycling is professional racing, the strength of the sport is in the millions who ride for fun, exercise, and recreation. According to Mike Weldon, who has coached Sue Novara, and Sheila and Roger Young, "The championship medal is always the icing on the cake. The strength and appeal of racing is in your clubs, in the families who train, race, and participate with their children. The next American Olympic champion will probably be the kid who arrives at the local velodrome with his stock bike, looking for some attention."

If Americans rediscovered the wheel a century ago, there is every indication that we are discovering it yet again. A hundred years ago the bicycle answered a nagging social and technological need. Men, women, and children were drawn to the boneshaker, the ordinary, and later the safety, by their desire to reject the plebeian art of walking. Moreover, the public quickly seized upon the bicycle as a machine capable of harnessing and multiplying man's power. No wonder writers in the 1890s were ecstatic about cycling man's potential to perform miracles of speed and distance. The bicycle was the instrument to raise the capabilities of man's legs and heart, a machine that would make him more efficient than the dolphin.

The bike boom ended, in a sense, when man decided he wanted to move faster than his legs could carry him, which was quite a normal development. In fact, many who had started with the bike, including Henry Ford, moved on to the automobile. As the internal combustion engine took over, the bicycle experienced a steady decline. First adult society discarded it, then the children. Whole generations grew up without riding bikes. As a form of final degradation, during the 1950s and 1960s, bicycles were considered by many to be toys for children, cumbersome things, more appropriately decorated than ridden. That bicycles could extend the heart and legs of man was a possibility lost.

Perhaps the last few decades will be judged by historians as a period in which society displayed little interest in the mobility of the body. It is not surprising that in the years that the bicycle was ignored or considered a children's toy, American schools were preparing generations of students for a lifelong commitment to spectator sports, such as baseball, football, and basketball, in which they would not or could not participate after their scholastic or collegiate careers. The hallmark of the physical fitness program was the sit-up, the push-up, the pull-up, with little attention to the heart and lungs. Important muscles atrophied, the wheels rusted.

But the wheels are again turning and some simple facts emerge. By 1980 it is estimated that there will be more bicycles than cars in America. Between 1898 and 1933 there were close to 150 bicycle tracks in the country. Massachusetts alone had tracks in Brockton, Athol, Springfield, Butterwood, Boston, Cambridge, Lowell, New Bedford, Worchester, Revere, Waltham, and Fall River. In the 1950s there were two tracks in the country. In 1976 there are veldromes in Flushing, New York; Trexlertown, Pennsylvania; East Point, Georgia; St. Louis, Missouri; Northbrook, Illinois; Kenosha, Wisconsin; Milwaukee, Wisconsin; San Jose and Encino, California; Alpenrose, Oregon; Redmond, Washington; and Detroit, Michigan. Dozens of others are in the planning or construction stage.

Similarly, grass-roots racing, conducted on running tracks, football fields, and auto speedways, is gaining in popularity. More

Allentown Call-Chronicle

Grass-track racing in Allentown, Pennsylvania before a crowd of 25,000 spectators.

and more towns and cities are permitting and encouraging clubs to conduct criteriums on local streets. Crowds of 25,000 and 20,000 respectively have attended grass-track races and cinder-track races in Allentown, Pennsylvania and Indianapolis, Indiana. Stock bike racing programs are making great strides (see Appendix). Bicycle racing is returning to the high schools and the colleges.

If facilities, spectators, and competitors represent a measure of a sport, then it can safely be said that bike racing has a bright future. Another measure of a sport, especially in these days of the armchair spectator, is its ability to capture the interest of man when, traditionally, his muscles sag and his spirit weakens. There are many people who know that cycling can contribute to the renewal of human energies, to the singing of the muscles, and to the dance of the body. Ed Delano knows.

Delano returned to the bike after a lapse of 39 years. In six months he could cycle over a hundred miles. At age 70 he cycled from Vacaville, California to Quebec City, Canada, just for fun. The same year he raced for 37 days with other veterans in Europe. Astonished at his lack of body fat and his magnificent performances, doctors believe he has reversed the aging process.

Delano knows the beauty of the legs against the wheel.

Postscript

FROM the conception to the completion of *American Bicycle Racing* strange and wonderful events have occurred in the cycling world, suggesting a new beginning in the muscular sport of track racing.

First, through a marvelous display of talent and determination, in the 1975 Pan-American Games, our track men made a foray into international sport. Overcoming substantial political and personal opposition, sprinter Steve Woznick earned a Gold in his event. His existential plunge into his own resources, his spectacular comeback from emotional ground zero due to faulty officiating, and his masterful sprint, gave character and a spirited nationalism to track racing.

Equally unexpected and exhilarating was the masterful work of the American Team Pursuiters who, riding on Woznick's emotional high, beat the heavily favored Colombian team for the Gold. Many feel that the team pursuit victory was possibly the most dramatic event in the history of American cycling. Surely all future American track victories will be computed from that date in 1975.

That the Pan-American Track team seemed to ride with the ripe edge of experience at their back was due to the masterful and courageous coaching of Jack Simes. Having reached the heights of European competition when American racing languished in the doldrums, Simes was determined that the current breed of racers would have better facilities and coaching. In addition, Simes wanted to give America her track champions.

Constructed at a time when American racing badly needed Olympic-type facilities, the Trexlertown velodrome and the local Pennsylvania community have given racing a home, a new beginning. In what must be a first in the growth period of an American sport, track racing has captured the imagination of the eastern Pennsylvania community. Thousands of converts to the sport have embraced the racing and the riders. Overnight, track racing has become a highly successful spectator sport. Sue Novara, Roger Young, Sheila Young, Jerry Ash, Gibby Hatton, Miji Reoch and other top riders are household words at the Trexlertown velodrome.

Fittingly, track racing, once the number one spectator sport in America, has returned in 1976.

Glossary

Handicap—riders all start at the same time, but at different marks around the velodrome. There are usually five or ten yards between riders with the faster riders starting behind the slower ones. Starting positions are determined by an official handicapper.

Scratch Race—otherwise known as a massed start race, it is one in which all riders start from the same mark.

Miss and Out—a race in which three or more riders compete and the last rider over the finish is withdrawn from the race. Riders may be eliminated every lap or every other lap depending upon the schedule stipulated before the race.

Point Race—a massed start race in which sprints for points are held on certain laps with the riders scoring the highest totals designated as first place, second place, etc.

Point to Point Race—same as a point race except that besides the regular designated sprints for points, the leader of each lap receives one point.

Team Race—othewise known as a Madison (named after Madison Square Garden where it developed), it is a race in which two or three contestants relay each other for the distance of the race.

Sprints—a series of heats of two, three, or four riders competing at a time in races usually not longer than one kilometer. Any number of riders may be entered but through the series of heats, eighth-finals, quarter-finals, and semifinals, they are eliminated until the finals, where the semifinal winners compete for first and second place.

Individual Pursuit Race—two riders starting equal distances apart on opposite sides of the track. The pursuit may be run until one rider catches the other and is declared the winner, or over a specified distance with the rider gaining the most ground on the other declared the winner.

Team Pursuit Race—same format as the individual pursuit except that it is usually run over a fixed distance of 4,000 meters and there are four contestants riding together as a team, each rider taking a turn setting the pace for the others.

Six-Day—originally a grueling, "nonstop" race for 144 hours; whoever traveled the farthest distance during the six days won the race. A rider was permitted to leave the track for a rest but only at the risk of losing mileage to his competitors. Because of heavy criticism, the one-man Six-Day was replaced by the two-man team race at the turn of the century. In later years, the emphasis on distance gave way to shorter racing sessions during the six day period consisting of fast racing and high-speed chases.

Peloton—literally means a squadron. It most frequently describes the cluster of riders bunched together at the head of a road race. Most of the riders in the peloton will be "sitting-in" behind the leaders where they are shielded from the wind. Here they can remain fresh and strong enough to initiate "breakaways" from the main body.

Criterium—a road race that is generally held in city streets or parks where the roads can be kept free of traffic. A criterium course is usually two miles or less and marked by short straights and tight turns which demand the utmost in bike handling.

Omnium—similiar to a decathalon, in which riders, by participating in a number of events (e.g., sprint, miss and out, kilometer), earn points. Ideally, such a race would determine the best all-around track man.

Appendix

United States Cycling Federation Stock Scholastic Bicycle Racing Program

The USCF, the official governing body for amateur bicycle racing in America, has adopted a stock bike racing program designed to meet the needs of the men, women, and children at the 57,000 schools and colleges in the country.

Bicycle racing is universal for all ages. Physical size has little bearing on the outcome of a race. Once the skill of riding efficiently and proficiently is acquired, it is a lifelong activity with innumerable fringe health benefits.

To participate in the program novice scholastic riders must be enrolled in junior high, senior high, or college, must have never held a racing license (USCF), and must use regular stock bikes.

A stock bike is one with a freewheel, hand brakes or coaster brakes, and drop center tires (clinchers). Bikes with tubulars (sew-ups) or fixed gear (no coasting) are not permitted. An acceptable bike must weigh 28 pounds. Gears will be limited to 72 inches or 226 inches per crank revolution.

Address inquiries to Scholastic Chairman, USCF, Inc., P.O. Box 480, East Detroit, Michigan 48021.

United States Cycling Federation Rider Divisions and Categories

Veteran Division—any male rider over the age of 40. Women do not have a veteran division.

Senior Division—any rider reaching his or her eighteenth birthday as of January 1 of the current year. There are four categories of senior riders:

Fourth Category—any senior making application for a USCF license for the first time.

Third Category—any junior passing from the junior to the senior division who has not qualified by his performance for second category or any fourth category rider of the previous year who has not qualified for second category.

Second Category—any senior who has placed among the first six in six or among the first three in three junior, fourth, or third category races.

First Category—any senior who has placed in the first six in six or the first three in three second category races.

Junior Division—any rider having reached his or her fourteenth birthday but not yet their eighteenth birthday as of January 1 of the current year.

Intermediate Division—any rider having reached his or her twelfth birthday but not yet their eighteenth birthday as of January 1 of the current year.

Midget Division—any rider having reached his or her ninth birthday but not yet their twelfth birthday as of January 1 of the current year.

To learn more about acquiring a United States Federation Racing License, contact your local bicycle club or the USCF office, P.O. Box 480, East Detroit, Michigan 48021.

Write to the following addresses for information about what's going on in particular velodromes:

Velodrome Locations

1. Alpenrose, Oregon. 5445 S. W. Childs Road, Lake Grove, Oregon 97034
2. Redmond, Washington. The Marymoor Velodrome. P.O. Box 15633, Seattle, Washington 98115
3. Northbrook, Illinois. 1441 Shermer Road, Northbrook, Illinois 60062
4. Kenosha, Wisconsin. 5843 Capri Lane, Morgan Grove, Illinois 60062
5. Detroit, Michigan. The Dorais Velodrome. 25897 Chippendale, Apt. A, Roseville, Michigan 48066
6. East Point, Georgia. Dick Lane Velodrome. 242 Superior Ave., Decatur, Georgia 30030
7. Flushing, New York. The Siegfried Stern Velodrome (or Kissena). New York City Park and Recreation Department, E. 36th Ave., New York City, New York 10021
8. San Jose, California. 17281 El Rancho Ave., Monte Sereno, California 95030
9. St. Louis, Missouri. 4701 Natural Bridge, St. Louis, Missouri 63113
10. Encino, California.
11. Trexlertown, Pennsylvania. Rodale Press, Inc. 33 East Minor St., Emmaus, Pennsylvania 18049
12. San Diego, California. 5779 Theta Place, San Diego, California 92120

Construction of Velodromes

Communities interested in building a velodrome should consult

Technical Bulletin Number Three, July 1975, published by the U.S. Bureau of the Interior, Southeast Regional Office. They should also consult a *Velo-News Velodrome Fact Sheet* published April 23, 1976. It contains important financial and technical information.

Copies of specific velodrome plans can be obtained from the USCF office, P.O. Box 480, East Detroit, Michigan 48021. These plans are for 33 1/3 and 400 meter velodromes only.

Alternate plans can be obtained from the City Engineer, City of East Point, Georgia 30344.

Communities are encouraged to work with service groups and local governments, who can greatly facilitate velodrome construction. Funds for a multi-purpose velodrome (running track on the apron, soccer and other activities in the infield) are available through the Land and Water Conservation Fund, administered by the Bureau of Outdoor Recreation. The Fund can pay up to 50 percent of the costs of a local recreation project. The Community Development funds administered by the Department of Housing and Urban Development, the recreation grant program administered by the Environmental Protection Agency, and the improvement programs of the National Park Service and the Corps of Engineers all represent potential sources of funds for the construction of a multi-purpose track.

Interested parties are also encouraged to visit existing velodromes, listed earlier in the Appendix.

Marking Out A Grass Track

Materials required are a long cord such as one used for a clothesline; some marker pegs; plus, of course, the normal line-maker machine, preferably filled with the modern rainproof "paint."

First, decide what size lap you need. To fit in a five-lap track you would require 66 yards for the length of the straight, plus 70 yards to allow for two radii of 35 yards each end, plus two widths of 20 to 22 feet for the actual track width each end; making 150 yards or so. Then you will have to allow clearance, say another ten feet each end.

When you have found out how much room you have to play with, start as follows: First, lay down your base line A-B (see diagram). This will be the length of your straights. You can now mark out your rectangle, in this order. Using a straight-edge, mark out the lines AC, AD, BE, and BF. Now carefully measure your radius-cord; mark it at the correct length allowing for fixing to a peg at A or B. As you walk around the semicircle, the machine with its paint must follow the end of the cord held close to the ground, thus completing the inner outline of the track. You can now mark the Sprinter's Line around the circumference, one yard out. Next mark in the Finish Line and other lines such as Pursuit Starts, Halfway line, etc., that you may require.

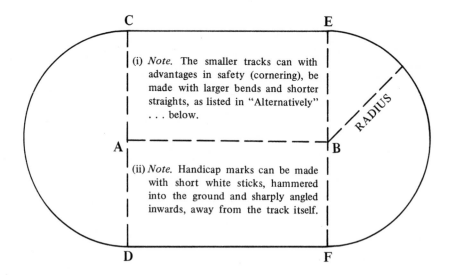

C   **E**

(i) *Note.* The smaller tracks can with advantages in safety (cornering), be made with larger bends and shorter straights, as listed in "Alternatively" . . . below.

A   **B**

(ii) *Note.* Handicap marks can be made with short white sticks, hammered into the ground and sharply angled inwards, away from the track itself.

D   **F**

Your track will have to fit into the field or ground that you intend to use, whether that be square, circular, or a long strip. Hence the various alternative sets of measurements below:

Four-laps-to-the-Mile.
Lap size, 440 yards.
Straights, 63 yards.
Radius of bends, 50 yards.

Five-laps-to-the-Mile.
Lap size, 352 yards.
Straights, 68 yards.
Radius of bends, 35 yards.

Alternate: Straight, 50 yards.
Radius, 40 yards.

Six-laps-to-the-Mile.
Lap size, 294 yards.
Straights, 52 yards.
Radius at bends, 30 yards.
Alternate: Straight, 36 yards.
Radius, 35 yards.

Seven-laps-to-the-Mile.
Straights, 49 yards.
Radius at bends, 27 yards.
Alternate: Straight, 32 yards.
Radius, 30 yards.

Bicycle Publications

Bicycle Spokesman
Dub Publishing Co.
119 East Palatine Rd.
Palatine, Illinois 60067

Bicycling
P.O. Box 3330
San Rafael, California 94902

Bike World
World Publications
Box 366
Mountain View, California 94040

These three publications cover road events, such as touring, and also contain technical information for the bike rider and racer. They are of interest to the general reader as well.

Velo-News
140 Elliot St.
Brattleboro, Vermont 05301

Competitive Cycling
P.O. Box 5453
Incline Village, Nevada 89450

Both of these publications are devoted to the sport of bicycle racing in the United States. Although *Velo-News* has somewhat of an East Coast bias, and *Competitive Cycling* favors the West, both cover nationwide events.

Cycling
161-166 Fleet St.
London, EC4P 4AA
England

This publication is primarily concerned with road racing in England and Europe. Fine coverage of indoor racing, especially the Six-Day, is also provided.

Selected Bibliography

Note: The following is a partial list of books and newspaper and magazine articles consulted in the preparation of this book, especially the first two chapters.

Bikes and Riders, James Wagenvoord, Avon Publishers, 1972.
Bicycle Racing, reprints from *Velo-News,* 1972–1974.
The Turned Down Bar, Nancy Neiman Burnnet, Dorrance, 1964.
Bicycling for Fun and Health, Lyle Kenyon Engel, Arco Publishing Co., 1975.
The Complete Book of Bicycling, Eugene A. Sloane, Trident Press, N.Y., 1970.
All About Bicycle Racing, World Publications, 1975.
The Fastest Bicycle Rider in the World, Marshall W. "Major" Taylor, reprinted by The Stephen Greene Press, 1972.
"Training and Feeding the Riders in a Six-Day Bicycle Treadmill," C. B. Davis, *Colliers,* 46:21, Feb., 1911.
"Racing for a Week," *Illustrated World,* 27:256, April, 1917.
"Infernal Grind," A. T. Goullet and C. J. McGuirk, *Saturday Evening Post,* 198:18–19, May 29, 1926.
"Six-Day Races Supreme Test of Grit," *Popular Mechanics,* 45:251–4, Feb., 1926.
"Jam in the Saucer," K. Crichton, *Colliers,* 95:26, Feb. 23, 1935.
"Daffy Whirl on Wheels; Six-Day Bicycle Race," *Literary Digest,* 120:32, Nov. 30, 1935.
"Six-Day Bicycle Racing with a Million Dollar Take," *Literary Digest,* 125:22, Jan. 8, 1938.
"Race to Nowhere; Six-Day Race," L. Davidson, *Rotarian,* 51:28–31, Dec., 1937.
"Six-Day Bike Racing in New York," *Life,* 24:57–58, March 29, 1948.
"A Brutal Exhibition," *New York Times,* 8, Dec. 11, 1897.
New York Times, 18, Dec. 11, 1898.
"Bicycling," *New York Times,* 19, Dec. 12, 1921.
"Major Taylor's Victory," *New York Times,* 5, Aug. 28, 1898.
"The Decline of the Bicycle," *New York Times,* 6, Sept. 13, 1900.
"Michael Defeated Taylor," *New York Times,* 5, Sept. 11, 1898.
"Cycling at the Garden," *New York Times,* 8, Jan. 9, 1898.
"Records of Wheelmen and Fast Horses Compared," *New York Times,* 8, Oct. 21, 1891.
"New York's Discarded Sports," *New York Times,* 10;18, Sept. 15, 1929.
"Bicycle Racing," *Encyclopedia of Sports,* Frank G. Menke, 5th Edition, 199-200.
New York Times, 3, Sept. 10, 1892.

"Six Teams Left in Race," *New York Times*, 2, Dec. 14, 1900.
"Cyclists' Weary Ride," *New York Times*, 2, Dec. 15, 1900.
"Professional Cycle Riders," *New York Times*, 21, March 4, 1900.
"Murphy's Achievement," *New York Times*, 6, July 5, 1899.
"Recalls Bike Ride at a Mile a Minute," *New York Times*, 21, June 27, 1934.
"Zimmerman Home Again," *New York Times*, 7, Nov. 13, 1894.
"Mrs. Minor Won the Race," *New York Times*, 7, Jan. 18, 1895.
"Miss Rhodes's Ten-Mile Record," *New York Times*, 6, Aug. 23, 1895.
"Defeat for Miss Hoyt," *New York Times*, 9, Oct. 19, 1900.
"Police Stop Miss Gast," *New York Times*, 8, Oct. 20, 1900.
"Mrs. Lindsay's 800 Miles," *New York Times*, 9, Oct. 19, 1899.
"Miss Yatman's Great Ride," *New York Times*, 8, Sept. 21, 1899.
"Woman Cyclist's Big Task," *New York Times*, 3, Sept. 11, 1899.
"Women's Bicycle Race," *New York Times*, 10, Nov. 21, 1900.
"Bicycles Against Time," *New York Times*, 3, Sept. 24, 1892.
New York Times, 18, Oct. 10, 1938.
"Johnson's New Cycle Record," *New York Times*, 3, Oct. 31, 1894.
"Zimmerman's New Training Track," *New York Times*, 8, Jan. 22, 1894.
"Johnson on Record Making," *New York Times*, 3, June 20, 1894.
"Mile on a Bicycle in 1:58 2–5," *New York Times*, 8, July 5, 1895.
"Racing, Speed and Endurance Records," *Riding High: The Story of the Bicycle*, Arthur Judson Palmer, New York: E. P. Dutton & Co., 169–189, 1956.
"Bicycle Racing," *The Encyclopedia of Sports*, Frank G. Menke, 4th Edition, 170–179, 1969.
"Bicycle Versus Thoroughbred," *Harpers Weekly*, 38:1977, Oct. 27, 1896.
Harpers Weekly, 39:1986, Jan. 12, 1897.
"20,000 Fans Watch Kramer's Last Ride," *New York Times*, 13, July 27, 1922.
"Kramer Rides Last Race in New York," *New York Times*, 10, July 26, 1922.
"Kramer is Crowned Bicycle Champion," *New York Times*, 11, Sept. 1, 1921.
"Kramer is Winner in Newark Opening," *New York Times*, 14, March 29, 1920.
"Zimmerman's Fast Mile," *New York Times*, 6, July 13, 1895.
"Cyclists Against Horsemen," *New York Times*, 6, Dec. 20, 1893.
"Six-Day Riders Split $75,000 in Prizes," *New York Times*, 35, Dec. 13, 1927.
"Jimmy Walthour Wins U.S. Road Bike Crown; Beats Benson Six Lengths After Point Tie," *New York Times*, 18, Sept. 12, 1927.
"Jimmy Walthour Wins Cycling Title," *New York Times*, 17, Aug. 31, 1927.

"Goullet Enters Six-Day Race; To Get $10,000, A Record Sum," *New York Times*, 17, Nov. 13, 1925.

"Goullet-Walthour Take Team Race," *New York Times*, 12, June 13, 1925.

"The Fast Rider Will Make an Attempt to Beat All Records," *New York Times*, 3, May 3, 1894.

" 'Zim' Back in America," *New York Times*, 6, Feb. 18, 1896.

"The Growth of Cycling," *New York Times*, 25, Jan. 5, 1896.

"What Makes Audrey Pedal?," Tiga Muk, *Sports Illustrated*, 31:22; 68–69, Nov. 24, 1969.

"Hell (And Heaven) on Wheels," Barry McDermott, *Sports Illustrated*, 43:18–20, Aug. 11, 1975.

"Young, Sheila," *The Lincoln Library of Sports Champions*, Sports Resources Co., Columbus, Ohio, 14:40–44, 1974.

"Fastest Legs in Two Leagues," Barry McDermott, *Sports Illustrated*, 39:20–1, Aug. 13, 1973.

"Linart Beats Wylie and McNamara," *Motorcycle & Bicycle Illustrated*, July 2, 1917, p. 33.

"Kramer Proves He Still Can Go Some," "Spencer Wins Three-Mile Open at Velodrome," *Motorcycle & Bicycle Illustrated*, Aug. 6, 1917, p. 37.

"Kramer Wins 25-Mile Bike Race," *Motorcycle & Bicycle Illustrated*, Aug. 13, 1917, p. 41.

"Kramer Burns the Wind—A Habit," *Motorcycle & Bicycle Illustrated*, Aug. 13, 1917, pp. 47; 49.

Index